Living Attention

Brennan - Transe.
Spinoza - Trasn of
offect aimpact

p.52 - v ✗✗
identify vs create.

SUNY series in Gender Theory

Tina Chanter, *editor*

Living Attention

On Teresa Brennan

Edited by

Alice A. Jardine
Shannon Lundeen
Kelly Oliver

STATE UNIVERSITY OF NEW YORK PRESS

Published by
STATE UNIVERSITY OF NEW YORK PRESS
ALBANY

© 2007 State University of New York

For information, address
State University of New York Press
194 Washington Avenue, Suite 305, Albany, NY 12210-2384

Production by Ryan Morris
Marketing by Anne M. Valentine

Library of Congress Cataloging-in-Publication Data

Living attention : On Teresa Brennan / edited by Alice A. Jardine, Shannon Lundeen, Kelly Oliver.
    p. cm. — (SUNY series in gender theory)
    Includes bibliographical references and index.
    ISBN-13: 978-0-7914-7079-4 (hardcover : alk. paper)
    ISBN-13: 978-0-7914-7080-0 (pbk : alk. paper)
    1. Brennan, Teresa, 1952– 2. Psychoanalysis and feminism. 3. Psychoanalysis.
4. Feminity. 5. Philosophy, Modern. I. Brennan, Teresa, 1952– II. Jardine, Alice.
III. Lundeen, Shannon. IV. Oliver, Kelly.

BF175.4.F45L58 2007
150.92—dc22   2006020751

10 9 8 7 6 5 4 3 2 1

Biographical Note on Teresa Brennan

———— ✎❀✎ ————

Teresa Brennan was born in Melbourne, Australia in 1952 and died February 3, 2003 as a result of a tragic hit-and-run. At the time of her death she held the Schmidt Distinguished Chair in the Humanities at Florida Atlantic University. Brennan received her bachelor's degree from the University of Sydney, a master's degree from the University of Melbourne, and a doctorate from Kings College, Cambridge University. Before coming to Florida Atlantic University, she was a visiting professor at Harvard, Brandeis, and Cornell Universities, New School for Social Research, the University of Amsterdam, the University of London, Oxford University, and the University of Melbourne.

Upon arriving at Florida Atlantic, Brennan founded an innovative doctoral program in the Comparative Studies Department. Designed by Brennan for scholars active in the public arena, the Public Intellectuals Program brought an impressive group of visiting scholars and activists to the university. Brennan also worked with the United Nations World Health Organization, where she was an invited philosopher.

Brennan's books include *Between Feminism and Psychoanalysis* (1989); *The Interpretation of the Flesh: Freud and Femininity* (1992); *History After Lacan* (1993); *Vision in Context: Historical and Contemporary Perspectives on Sight* (edited with Martin Jay, 1996); *Exhausting Modernity: Grounds for a New Economy* (2000); *and Globalization and Its Terrors: Daily Life in the West* (2003). Her last book, *The Transmission of Affect*, was published posthumously by Cornell University Press in 2004.

Contents

Acknowledgments

———— ❧❦❧ ————

ALICE A. JARDINE: I am sincerely grateful to the faculty and staff of Women, Gender, and Sexuality Studies at Harvard University, and especially to the Chair of WGS, Afsaneh Najmabadi, for their generous support of the memorial conference in Teresa's honor held at Harvard on May 1, 2004. I am grateful to my co-editors, Shannon Lundeen and Kelly Oliver, for their spirit and determination to make this volume happen. I want to express my sincere admiration for the many friends and colleagues from around the world who have spoken at one or more of the conferences and panels organized in Teresa's honor since her untimely death. I especially want to thank Teresa's daughter, Sangi; Angela Williams, Sangi's guardian angel; my many priceless friends; and my own dear Anna for all their love and moral support during the time this volume was being compiled. Finally, thank you, Teresa, for teaching me so much about what really matters in our short lives on earth, and especially about how to give and receive a quality of Living Attention that can really make a difference.

Shannon Lundeen: I would like to thank my co-editors, Kelly Oliver and Alice Jardine, for giving me the opportunity to work on such an inspiring and robust collection of essays on Teresa Brennan. I would also like to thank Teresa for her unwavering commitments to feminist theory, social justice, and radical thinking and activism, all of which are evident in the scholarship that she has left us. To each of the authors in this volume, I would like to express my gratitude for not only your insightful, critical essays, but also for your receptivity, flexibility, and promptness during the editing stages of the book. Finally, I would like to express my appreciation to my family and friends for supporting me in this and all other projects that I've taken on.

Kelly Oliver: Thanks to Elizabeth Grosz for helping to organize the Teresa Brennan Memorial Symposium at Stony Brook University, Manhattan, October 2–4, 2003. Thanks to all of the participants, some of whom have contributed to this volume. Shannon Lundeen, Michael Sigrist, and Julie Sushytska provided invaluable assistance for that event. Thanks to Shannon Lundeen who has also done the "lion's share" of the editing for this volume and kept us all on schedule. A special thanks to Tina Chanter and Jane Bunker for their encouragement and confidence in this project. Finally, thank you Teresa for your inspiring work and life, which continue to engage us.

Introduction

❧❧❧

Shannon Lundeen

THE ESSAYS IN THIS collection are a tribute to the significance of the work of Teresa Brennan. Although the body that she so gracefully and vivaciously inhabited is gone, Teresa Brennan's intellect, spirit, and energy are very much present in her scholarly work and the engagements with that work in this volume. Throughout her work, from her first book *The Interpretation of the Flesh* to her most recent, *The Transmission of Affect*, Teresa develops an original and revolutionary notion of energetics that she applies to some of the most pressing social issues of our time: relations between men and women, our relation to the environment and pollution, contemporary diseases, and globalization. Like her life, her work is not traditional or ordinary. It shakes things up and gives us new insights into our most profound relationships with each other, to time and space, and to global capital. Her work has transformed feminist psychoanalytic theory, economic theory, and the way that we conceive of the relationship between psychoanalysis and social theory. The essays in this volume demonstrate the importance and creativity of Teresa Brennan's life and thought and the gravity and significance of our loss.

Alice Jardine opens the volume with an essay that traces the development of Brennan's thought from her first book, *The Interpretation of the Flesh* (1992), to her last, *The Transmission of Affect* (2004). Although a constant interlocutor, collaborator, colleague, and dear friend of Teresa's, Jardine had not read one of Brennan's books until after her death in February of 2003. As Brennan's thoughts turned from the individual psyche and its interpersonal relations to a social psyche and its global implications, Jardine turns from the Teresa she knew in private and personal exchanges to the public and scholarly Brennan revealed in her publications. Jardine notes that in their personal exchanges, Brennan had always been plagued by the question "What is to be done now?" (p. 2) and she finds that the development of Brennan's thought over the course of her oeuvre was driven by this same question. For those unfamiliar with the extent and breadth of Teresa Brennan's thought and

scholarship, "A Surplus of Living Attention," provides an astute and comprehensive introduction to Brennan's work.

In her first book, *The Interpretation of the Flesh* (1992), Brennan lays the groundwork for what she calls the "foundational fantasy" and in her chapter, "Living A Tension," Kelly Oliver examines the conceptual and theoretical trajectories of this fantasy throughout Brennan's subsequent texts. The foundational fantasy begins with an infant's hallucination that it is both self-contained and in control of its primary caregiver. As an illusion of self-containment, the foundational fantasy grounds the myths of the ego's boundedness, of women's tractability and corresponding notion of femininity, and of the inexhaustibility of the earth's resources. It may seem, based on her analysis of the foundational fantasy, that Brennan advocates strategies of mobility over and against strategies of containment. However, Oliver points to those places in Brennan's work where her assessments of attempts to bind and contain things, energies, people, resources, etcetera become ambivalent. Oliver examines and critiques Brennan's simultaneous calls for economic self-containment, on the one hand, and personal mobility, circulation, and exchange of psychic energies and affects, on the other. It is the latter, the intersubjective exchange of energies and affects upon which Brennan's theory of the drives is based, that Oliver hails as "revolutionary" in Brennan's work.

One particular phenomenon that Brennan focuses on throughout the development of her drive-theory is the projection and exchange of negative affect. According to Brennan, negative affects, which always come from outside rather than from within, have dire and dangerous consequences for the world at large: their constant projection and escalating circulation accounts for the depletive nature of global capitalism as well as the historical development of an exhausted and exploited feminine position. Although she notes that Brennan's theory of the transmission of affect is radically significant for psychoanalytic theory, feminism, and economics, Oliver challenges and unsettles Brennan's associations of negative affect with what is outside and positive affect with what is inside in light of Brennan's own critique of psychical, physical, and energetic containment in psychoanalytic theory. Oliver argues that in the face of all-consuming forces of globalization and the normalization of the "feminine position" for women, Brennan seems only to offer us repression of the negative. Exploring the implications of Brennan's concept of the foundational fantasy and understanding of the drives for ethical and feminist theories, Oliver points us to the lack of strategies of resistance in Brennan's work and charges us to "acknowledge the positive effects of the transmission of affect in relationships that create a surplus of living attention and energy" (p. 22).

In the third chapter, Robyn Ferrell takes up the figure of time difference to explore the theme of geopolitics of philosophy that Ferrell sees as central

to Brennan's work. Contextualizing her essay within a "time of globalization," as a fellow Australian, Ferrell explores what time difference in this context means for differences between the U.S. and Australia, between 1993 (the year Ferrell first met Brennan and Brennan's second book, *History After Lacan*, was published) and now, between herself and Brennan. "Time Difference" situates Brennan's work, specifically *History After Lacan*, within the history of Australian materialism in order to explore the political and scholarly tensions created by Brennan's work in the Australian academy which, she contends, is often "obscured by the supposedly international forum of philosophical work" (p. 25). Systematically working through the theses that Brennan puts forth in *History After Lacan*, Ferrell illuminates Brennan's theoretical objectives in an entirely new way by closely attending to differences not only of time but also of place and space between Brennan's innovations in psychoanalytic theory and the canon of Australian materialism.

In the fourth chapter, Anne O'Byrne relates Brennan's work directly to that of Heidegger. Brennan acknowledges her indebtedness to Heidegger's undermining of the subject's privileged place in ontology. But as O'Byrne delineates in "Heidegger after Brennan," she frequently distances herself from Heidegger's level of abstraction and his privileging of the ontological over the ontic. Although this is a familiar critique, O'Byrne insists that Brennan's particular critique of Heidegger is novel in its focus on three points: 1) the foundational fantasy; 2) the foundational fantasy's relation to technological development; and 3) the figure and role of the mother in the foundational fantasy (p. 34). Elucidating the connections between Brennan and Heidegger, O'Byrne details Heidegger's work on generation as well as his critique of foundations and explains the way in which his work on these concepts proved to be both a springboard for Brennan's development of her theory of the foundational fantasy as well as an object of her critique. Reading Heidegger *after* Brennan, O'Byrne argues, compels us to take a new look at spatiality and origin which, in turn, leads us to a new reading of "generation" that takes us beyond Heidegger's conceptualization of generation as disembodied. Although O'Byrne provocatively challenges certain components of Brennan's reading of Heidegger, she uses Brennan to develop a richer account of Heideggarian concepts. Placing Brennan in dialogue with Heidegger as well as contemporary Heidegger scholars, O'Byrne ultimately provides a rich account of Dasein's spatiality that is informed by Brennan's "fleshy" conceptualization of the process of generation.

In the fifth chapter "Repressed Knowledge and the Transmission of Affect," Susan James invites us to investigate modern philosophical discussions of affective exchange in order to compare such discussions to Brennan's theory of the transmission of affect. James discusses the way in which Brennan's theory of the transmission of affect, which holds that affects are transmitted from one person to another through the body (primarily through hormonal exchanges), directly undermines a masculinist notion of a self-contained and independent subject who is shored up by the dualisms of subject/object and mind/body. Brennan's argument suggests that we have repressed the fact of transmission in order to maintain this notion of the self as a discretely-bounded, autonomous subject. To overcome this repression, we need to cultivate what Brennan calls discernment, as James explains it, "the power to feel with our bodies the difference between transmitted and non-transmitted affects" (p. 48). Like Oliver, James is concerned with both the role of repression in Brennan's theory as well as the function of the inside/outside dichotomy in structuring her discussion of the various modes of affective transmission. James critically examines Brennan's notions of discernment, repression, and affective transmission against a backdrop of debates about "passionate exchange" among modern theorists such as Spinoza, Malebranche, Hume, and Smith. Similar to Oliver's contention in chapter 2, James suggests that Brennan places too much emphasis on the transmission of negative affects and sacrifices any concern with the transmission of positive affects. James offers us a historical narrative of the discussion of the transmission of affect that she believes is missing from Brennan's account and in so doing she aims to clarify Brennan's positions on the ego, its repressions, and affective transmission.

Sustaining the discussion of Brennan's work on the transmission of affect, Charles Shepherdson, in "Emotion, Affect, Drive: For Teresa Brennan," details the way in which Brennan's theory of affect both builds upon and departs from Freud's notion of affect (as developed in "Mourning and Melancholia") and Lacan's notion of affect that is connected to the concepts of drive and jouissance. While James uses the terms *affect* and *passion* interchangeably in the previous chapter, Shepherdson introduces a distinction between affect and emotion that he maintains arises as a conceptual consequence of Lacan's understanding of the distinction between the symbolic order and jouissance. Although Freud did not employ this distinction in his work, Shepherdson argues that calling attention to the border between jouissance and the symbolic leads to an understanding of *affect* as (what Freud would have called) a charge of energy and *emotion* as a symbolic phenomenon. With this distinction in mind, Shepherdson asks of Brennan's theory whether it is affect or, in fact, emotion that gets transmitted between subjects. Moreover, Shepherdson asks how, in Brennan's theory of the drives, we are to distinguish symbolic transmission from the transmission of jouissance. Working through Brennan's understanding of the exchange and intersubjective transmission of energies, Shepherdson demonstrates the way in which her work could be sharpened by a distinction between affect and emotion where language and the flesh are inextricably linked.

Kalpana Rahita Seshadri's "After Teresa Brennan" continues the previous two chapters' critical examination of Brennan's theory of the exchange and transmission of affect. Originally written as a response letter to Brennan regarding her manuscript of the now posthumously published *Transmission of Affect* (2004), Seshadri's essay is as theoretically incisive as it is personally moving. Seshadri carefully attends to what she sees as Brennan's "stunning" and "surprising" interventions into and revisions of the psychoanalytic theory of affects, namely Brennan's discussion of the relationship between affect and ideas and the intersubjective functioning of affects. Yet she also enumerates what she believes to be weaknesses in the manuscript which, Seshadri maintains, emanate from Brennan's failure to see the death drive as producing anything that is not negative. Seshadri suggests that a more nuanced understanding of the death drive might lead Brennan to conclude that negative affects and drives do not always function to thwart positive personal and political intersubjective relations but instead produce and encourage them. Throughout the letter/chapter, Seshadri rigorously questions the implications of Brennan's theory of the transmission of affect for philosophical and psychoanalytic concepts ranging from intentionality to the unconscious.

In "*Ubuntu* and Teresa Brennan's Energetics," Drucilla Cornell develops the sense of ethical responsibility that emanates from Brennan's plea to create an economy of generosity that would undermine the economy of scarcity through which global capital operates. A generous economy would demand a new way of living together and a new way of utilizing and replenishing the earth's resources on local and global scales. But what sort of ethical imperative would compel us to devise such an economy? Cornell brings our attention to the South African concept of *ubuntu* which, she suggests, provides us with a notion of ethical responsibility that is in line with Brennan's call for an economy of generosity. Designating humanity as interdependent, interactive, intergenerational, intercorporeal, and communal, *ubuntu* is an ethical configuration that, Cornell claims, is unparalleled in the Western philosophical canon. Because it confounds any notion of self-containment or self-generation, Cornell argues that *ubuntu* has the capacity to undermine the necessity and pervasiveness of the foundational fantasy and to illuminate the way in which we might begin to create an economy of sustenance and generosity.

In Gillian Beer's chapter, "What's Not Seen," she shifts our attention to Brennan's endeavors to undermine the dualism of mind and body that, among other modern philosophical tenets, shores up the foundational fantasy. Beer concentrates on the way in which literature and poetic thinking work to rebut the mind-body split and she outlines the places in Brennan's work where this is evident. Drawing a connection between Brennan's work on vision and the literary dimension of thought, Beer argues that in their call to what is not there and in their dependence on what is not seen, vision and literature work in similar fashion to confound the boundaries between the mind and the body, knowledge and experience, intellect and matter. Beer contextualizes Brennan's disruption of the mind/body split within a centuries-long debate that has garnered the participation of thinkers from a number of various fields and academic disciplines ranging from ethics to neuroscience. Exploring the relationship between knowledge, death, experience, and writing, Beer invites us to see Brennan's writing—scholarly, literary, and poetic—as something that "holds experience steady past death and allows it to find expression in an assurance [for which] the mind-body split cannot account" (p. 105).

In the tenth chapter, Jane Gallop continues this discussion of the connection between writing and death as it appears in and is elicited by reading Brennan's last book, *The Transmission of Affect*. Brennan's last manuscript was not yet "finished" at the time of her death. In "Reading Brennan," Gallop explores how this fact resonates with the way in which Brennan thought about writing and finishing. While in the third chapter, Ferrell brought up the question of time difference in relation to Brennan's writing in the Australian academy, Gallop raises the question of enough time in Brennan's life and work. There, she traces the connections between Brennan's scholarly work on time (her preference for speed), her attitude toward time (never wanting to be rushed, always assuming people and planes would simply wait for her if she was late), and her anxiety over "finishing" (she rarely thought a book or paper was finished and oftentimes her assistants had to forcibly take her "unfinished" books away from her). In a critical analysis of Brennan's preference for speed, Gallop offers an insightful and instructive account of the connections between this privileging of rapidity and the labor of writing, death, the blockages of the foundational fantasy, and Brennan's theory of the transmission of affect.

The final chapter of this volume, "Can We Make Peace? For Teresa Brennan," is an essay that Julia Kristeva has dedicated to Teresa Brennan. Kristeva originally presented the paper in 2002 at the 6th International Forum of the Universal Academy of Cultures in Paris. In her essay on whether we can, in fact, make peace at a time in which conflict and terror are so prevalent around the globe, Kristeva tenders a response to the question that Jardine tells us in chapter 1 was ever-pressing for Teresa: "What is to be done now?" Thus, Kristeva's contribution properly rounds out this collection on Brennan's life and work by returning us to one of the primary questions that fueled her projects. Kristeva turns to the Catholic tradition, to Freud, Kant, and to Arendt and explores the answers offered by each as to whether and how we can make peace. She argues that what we suffer from most today and what keeps us in a perpetual state of conflict and unrest is the loss of the language of life: "The love of life eludes us; there is no longer a discourse for it" (p. 121). Renewing the desire for life is essential, Kristeva maintains, for envisioning and more importantly, imagining peace. According to Kristeva eliciting the desire for and love of life can be accomplished by doing what many of Brennan's texts have done, by inscribing the question of peace into philosophy, literature, and the arts.

As the last contribution to the volume, Susan Buck-Morss's essay offers Teresa and the readers of this volume a eulogy that resonates with the radical political thinking that Brennan has always embraced. "A Eulogy for Teresa Brennan" offers us an epistemological manifesto for a different kind of think-ing and writing on the part of progressive intellectuals. The essay issues an inspiring call to the readers of this volume for the production of rigorous polit-ical thought combined with activism. Since, for Brennan, activism does not have to be separate from but rather can be imbued in writing, Buck-Morss's piece is a fitting tribute to a public intellectual who was committed to going beyond writing to change the world.

CHAPTER ONE

A Surplus of Living Attention

Celebrating the Life and Ideas of Teresa Brennan

———— ❧❧ ————

Alice A. Jardine

> The point is that in order to act upon the world, any being needs
> an identity, and living attention from within if not from without.
>
> —Brennan, *The Interpretation of the Flesh*

Introduction

LET ME BEGIN WITH a confession: Over the course of my twenty years of
friendship with Teresa Brennan, I lived and breathed her books; but I fiercely
resisted *reading* them, until after her death. I have asked myself why and have
yet to come up with a satisfactory response. But I am not alone, a lot of folks
resist reading the books or looking at the art of their nearest and dearest
friends. I mean, what if you hated it! Can deep friendship ever really recover
from that? But the best reason I can come up with so far is that for twenty
years I felt as if I *was* reading them. Teresa and I lived and talked and breathed
theories about the world; and yet even as we analyzed everything and everyone in our lives, daily, for twenty years, I resisted reading her books. That is,
until that very day in February of 2003 when I left her already cold, abandoned body in that strange South Florida funeral home. That was the day
I began to read her books. Everything. Every word. In chronological order.
From the "Foundational Fantasy" of *The Interpretation of the Flesh* (1992),
through her diagnosis of the "Social Psychosis" dividing our world violently
into the "servers" and the "served" in *History After Lacan* (1993), then on
to the deadening effects of techno-capital's race to destruction in *Exhausting
Modernity* (2000) toward all the ways in which we are killing ourselves not
so softly in *Globalization and Its Terrors* (2003). I have only recently emerged

1

from the clarity and hope of the last book completed before Teresa's murder, *The Transmission of Affect* (2004). I have now read them all—one of my ways of mourning no doubt.

But my reaction goes beyond the personal. I have been stunned by the cumulative vision of these books, an unexpected gift of insight offered to those of us still committed to making the world a better place. I am sorry that it took me so long to read them; but then, maybe that's in part why I was able to garner such a surplus of living attention from Teresa while alive.

So what do I do with these books? Where do I start with these volumes of self-assured prose, this forthright insistence on the imperative of the big picture, the grand meta-narrative, this utter disregard for disciplinary boundaries, this fluctuating emotional intensity, moving back and forth seamlessly between *Star Wars* jokes and the most intricate and serious complexities of psychoanalytic, economic, and political theories? How do I proceed when the living voice has unexpectedly gone silent, almost as if in defiance of the theory itself? What is to be done?

Work is to be done. Self-assuredly. Insistently. With living attention. Exactly what she would want us to do.

I am going to attempt to work through, chronologically and somewhat summarily, what Teresa always called "her theory." Her theory of what, you might ask? Of nothing more and nothing less than what we always called "the fix the world is in." "Work through" is too strong. I am neither a philosopher nor a political theorist, but rather a student of literature and the arts. What I'm going to do here then is to tell a story. I'm going to tell the theoretical story I have read in the five published books as inflected by my experience of her surplus of living attention. Those readers who know me and my work will understand that I am not (even as a storyteller) naïve enough to present my theoretical fable as Teresa's theoretical truth. But it is a beginning. It is one way of enticing all of you to read more of Teresa Brennan. It is my way of asking what was always Teresa's and my primary question together: *What is to be done now?*

The Interpretation of the Flesh

Teresa has argued that the formation of femininity and the energetic exploitation at work on the interpersonal level between men and women are intrinsically linked. In the first instance, we are talking about the *micro*-cosmic concerns first outlined in *The Interpretation of the Flesh: Freud and Femininity* (1992). There she takes Freud's "riddle of femininity" very seriously and proposes a radical metapsychology of her own invention, one meant to address the economic, spatial, and interactive levels of psychic organization. In short, she argues that in order to become subjects and act upon the world, men have resorted to "unloading," projecting all negative affects and aggressions upon some "other"—even beyond the infantile fantasies of destroying the mother—in such a way that the process of positioning that "other" to acquiesce to the projection has historically required the formation of a *normative femininity*: the normal (read: pathological) state of Western Womanhood.

Women have largely been forced to passively accept that projection in exchange for recognition (identity) and security (protection). Teresa asks: What if feminism has been largely the rejection of that projection, allowing many women to begin to dump Western femininity's historically negative effects on our curiosity, our intelligence and our activity? What happens then as women's demands for recognition and their needs for security undergo radical historical and geographical transformations? Teresa was acutely attuned to the necessity of thinking through both the gains and the losses—the unsettling consequences—of the end of "true patriarchy."

History After Lacan

Teresa argued that the "foundational fantasy" she described on the psychical level in her first book has, over time, triggered a more general social psychosis in the West, which is now predominant and threatening the entire globe. The psychical fantasy of woman at the core of the foundational fantasy, having triggered a more generalized social psychosis involving the massive exploitation of energy at the socio-historical level, has particularly, over the twentieth century slowly but surely divided the world into the "servers" and the "served"—an untenable equation on an untenable scale. In this second instance, we are talking about the *macro*-cosmic social psychosis that Teresa began to outline in *History After Lacan* (1993).

The central character in this social psychosis is the ego, "an ego which is just as social and collective as the psychosis it underpins" (Brennan 1993, 3). The "ego's era" began in the seventeenth century and continues today, but its processes have accelerated and expanded right along with technology and capital. In fact, sexual difference (at the core of the foundational fantasy) has, over time, been homogenized across race, religion, and class, flipping over into a world-wide, historically unprecedented division between the shapers and the shaped, the aggressors and the pacified. We all get caught up in this generalized psychosis no matter how hard we resist because of the power of the ego's insistence on "fixed points":

> In *The Interpretation of the Flesh*, I wrote that the ego depends on fixed points because it depends on its identifications with others, and ideas, to maintain its sense of its individual distinctness, or identity. These identifications involve the image the ego receives from the other, an image which remains still or constant in relation to the movement of life. Psychically we need

these fixed points, but they also hold us back . . . In this book I argue that the fixed points of the psyche are paralleled and reinforced by the construction of commodities in the social world: psychical fixed points block the mobility of psychical energy; the technologically fixed points of commodities, unless they are constructed with care, block the regeneration of nature and natural energy. (ibid., xii)

. . . [T]echnological expansion . . . is the means whereby the ego is able to secure the "reversal" in knowledge, as it makes the world over in its own image. It is also, and this is critical to the dynamics of the ego's era, a means of generating continuous economic insecurity and anxiety over survival in the majority, and guarantees their dependence on those identified with the dominant ego's standpoint. (ibid., 44)

Through the proliferation of fixed points and the speeding up of capital's expansion via the development of technology, the profit imperative creates a spatio-temporal speed-up in the production of commodities. That speed-up then binds more and more energy to the commodities produced. Since nature is the ultimate source of all value and energy, the constantly increasing speed of capital—and its production of commodities as "fixed points"—diminishes nature at an unbelievable pace. This speed-up alters *physis* itself in the process, "adjusting" the inbuilt logic of nature and the spacio-temporal continuum to suit the will of ego-era capital. The value and energy of *nature and its space* is attacked in the name of *technology and its time:*

The point here is simply that in order to satisfy the demands of large-scale production, more and more of nature has to be destroyed. In this sense production under capitalism is consumption, not production; it gobbles that which is already there, and gives nothing back but waste. Its form of transforming labour is not the same as that which marks other modes of the production process, in that capital is only concerned about reproducing the natural substances that are the irreplaceable conditions of its own existence . . . (Brennan 1993, 138)

Everything speeds up, even so-called "natural" processes. We breed pigs that get fat so fast, they can't walk; young turkeys get such huge breasts, they can't mate. The cloning or artificial engineering of animals and plants speeds things up even more; we consume more, faster, easier. This elaborate phantasmatic frenzy, this speeding up at all levels does not, paradoxically, lead the West toward its stated goals:

The price paid for speeding things up is a price paid by overall productivity, and hence overall long-term profit. There should be a decline in long-term profit to the extent that commodities embody less real substance, and this they must do as they become degraded of substance. Take the giant, airy *lu: galletia?*

American strawberry. Genetically recombined for improved size, and grown from degraded soil, it looks great and tastes . . . like nothing. In the medium term, even its comparative price has fallen. It is a symptomatic postmodern commodity: seeming wonderful, yet it has literally less substance, and hence less value. None the less, its price increased in the short term with the speed of its deceptively luscious production. (Brennan 1993, 141)

By the end of her second book, Teresa has begun to ask more direct questions about how this speedy, toxified environment literally gets inside subjects who then act in strikingly similar ways to reproduce it—subjects who seem to be overcome with what she calls "unremittingly controlled willfulness" working frantically to produce a "grey mirror of sameness." This question begins to point toward what many see as Teresa's most academically radical theory, that of an *interactive economy of energies*—energies that spring up not only inside but around and through the individuals through which they course. Here she challenges all of us in the academy to lose our elitism and pay more sustained attention to history and culture beyond our own fixed points of reference:

Now the notion that there is a conative, energetic force coursing through and activating individual subjects and their living environment is not new. It was with us before, and is appearing now. In its naturalistic form, it enjoyed a certain popularity in the guise of pantheism, Romanticism, *Naturphilosophie*. It attained some respectability in Spinoza's name. Today it is prominent in the cosmic consciousness theories that inform the New Age culture, and which spill over into the theories of the German Greens . . . In New Age culture especially, the idea of a connecting force survives, but it survives on miserable arguments, and is always assumed to be good. The idea also survives in popular culture, where notions of energetic connections between beings are seen as both beneficent and malign. The idea has returned in a series of blockbuster films ('May the force be with you') and in writers ranging from Arthur C. Clarke to Toni Morrison. Morrison's *Beloved* was revolutionary, ahead of academic time, in writing of psychical feelings and forces which were not self-contained but crossed between individuals. (Brennan 1993, 81)

Exhausting Modernity

So far, Teresa has argued that the psychical fantasy of woman, triggering the massive social psychosis of the Western ego's era, moving everyone toward the desire for a form of willful subjectivity and instant commodities to be delivered at one's immediate command—a desire that has in turn led to violent levels of ethnocentrism and ecological devastation—has led to the need for nothing less than *a permanent state of war*. "[For . . .] we shall [all] continue to want to be subjects. We will want to be subjects even against our wills, because there is a politics of exhaustion being played out in relation to the fantasy on a global scale" (Brennan 1993, 186).

In the third instance, we are talking about a politics of exhaustion that Teresa began to outline in *Exhausting Modernity: Grounds for a New Economy* (2000). Already, in *History After Lacan*, the world Teresa described was getting more scary and the necessity as well as possibility for resistance more insistent and more explicit:

> [In this world] we will want to be subjects to garner the energy needed to move—whether it is through the attentive recognition and labour of others, or those expensive "labour-saving devices." The consequence of living in the high tech built environment is that one almost has to be a subject to repel its deadening effects. As I hope I have shown, these deadening effects are deceptive: the world from which they emanate appears to be a world of more rapid motion, with a rapid pulse that can for a time be taken as energy itself, as it speeds up one's conscious tempo. But the price of this temporary excitement will be paid somewhere. Even if it is not paid by the subject who benefits, the deadening effects of this environment more and more make each and everyone an object. That is what lack of love, in Eagleton's terms a political as well as personal affair, will always do. So will lack of connection. (Brennan 1993, 186–187)

According to Teresa, one must fight this lack of connection at every level—from the challenges of interpersonal life to the efforts of organized resistance. The struggles on the inside must match the struggles on the outside; both call for *an alteration of scale*. This is the "new economy"—the truly third way—that Teresa articulates with a sense of impending doom because, she argues:

> [M]odernity is producing a more complete and final form of death. Its victorious economy, capitalism, is turning biodegradable life into a form in which it can generate nothing. Once this is plain, it will also be apparent that judgement, in one sense of that term, is anything but metaphorical. One of the most ancient senses we can give to the idea of "judgement" is, "that which rights the balance." By binding more and more of life in a form in which it cannot reproduce life, capitalism, and a complicit modernity, disturbs an ecological balance. How that balance is righted remains to be determined. But there are now few on the planet who dispute that the balance needs to be corrected in this beleaguered present. (Brennan 2000, 2)

It is here, I think, that Teresa comes the closest she has so far to revealing her most private and controversial cards—her unfailing optimism due mostly to her unfailing belief in a God(dess), a fascination with the histories and stories of world religions equal only to her bitter disappointment in the modern Christian Church.

optimistic

The rise of capital, the downgrading of nature, the victory of death over life, of the Devil over God, as the Foundational Fantasy is intensified through modernity. This is the dark vision that leads Teresa back once again to her daring theory of the relationship between energetics and economics as being a different pathway for "thinking our way out of this mess":

> It is in this time [the past three centuries] that a modern and profoundly Western economy has made omnipotent fantasies into realities. My argument here is that while the fantasy pre-exists modernity, its force in the social order is intensified by modernity. The modern economy, and any social order in which the religious and other ethical constraints on the fantasy are removed, increases the extent to which that fantasy is acted out socially. Hence it increases the extent of commodification, and, accordingly, the significance of money. In turn, the fantasy's social enactment increases its hold over the human psyche and the power of the desires born through that fantasy. In explaining this dialectic, we are drawn first to energetics, then to economics. (Brennan 2000, 9–10)

Teresa goes on to underline, what for me, in many ways is her most important argument: that for any theory to have strong, sustainable explanatory power for a large number of people, *it must have experiential appeal*. Why do middle-aged men leave their middle-aged wives for ever younger women? Or, more generally, why can't any of us wait? We kick the vending machines (lightly perhaps), yell at the waiters (even if only under our breath), endlessly upgrade the internet connection (late at night, when no one's watching). We the consumers, as the producers of modern capital, make it all happen but we want it to happen more quickly, more seamlessly, more automatically. All that takes is money. So we work harder. So why *is* everyone in the first world so exhausted?

> This is a world where inertia, exhaustion and the sense of running hard to stay in the same place mark everyday life. They are as much a mark of the present depression as environmental degradation. There is a terrible tiredness around, a sense of having no energy, or of energy departing. In fact one can only understand this experience, and the connections between psychical myths and fantasies and the course of capital, if one takes energy into account . . . (Brennan 2000, 11–12)

Globalization and Its Terrors

Toward the end of her third book, Teresa begins to move slowly toward our own very present moment and its enactment on a global scale of what she has described thus far. That enactment she calls *globalization*.

It is in her fourth book that Teresa begins, I think, to address her critics' accusations of ethnocentrism. This was an accusation she could never understand given her personal and intellectual preference for residing in non-Western countries and her conviction that most if not all of her most valued concepts come from non-first world cultures—most centrally, her embrace of human subjectivities that are not excessively defined by the Western subject/object paradigm, it's necessarily ego-centered fantasies, its violent acts of emotional dumping, and its repression of what she will come to term "the transmission of affect."

According to Teresa's argument, it is clear that the force of the "foundational fantasy" is greatest in the West, not so much because that's where she was born, but because of the specificities of the history of the foundational fantasy's reproduction and exponential growth in capitalistic modernity. She was convinced that, while one can still even today, experience other forms of being outside of the so-called first world, Western subject/object models can take hold quickly enough anywhere—whether in Asia, Africa, South America, or (her favorite defense and illustration) Eastern Europe, as capital moves in new and different directions, often to the direct detriment of those embracing it in the hope that their lives will improve. In the fourth instance, Teresa provides what she calls her "empirical companion book" to all the others: *Globalization and its Terrors: Daily Life in the West* (2003). This "empirical volume" proclaims its function loudly, right on the cover of the book:

> It has long been realized that the poorer countries of the South have paid for the unstoppable onward rush of globalization in the exploitation of their natural and human resources. Recent events have made it clear that there is a price to be paid in the West as well . . . the evidence already exists showing that globalization has for years been harming not only the poor of the Third World but also its alleged beneficiaries in the affluent West . . . the speeding up of contemporary capitalism—in which space is substituted for time—means that neither the environment nor the people who live in it are given the opportunity to regenerate . . . this leads directly to pollution-induced, immune-deficient and stress-related disease.

There is another paragraph in this clever marketing come-on (i.e., globalization is really about "you" not "them"):

> *With much talk of religious judgment on either side in the current global conflict . . . global reasoned analysis combined with local action counters economic exploitation. Left to itself, such exploitation produces environmental catastrophe, turning judgment from a prophecy to a probability.*

Ortho gin quote

Our bodies

This explicit political and spiritual outing of where Teresa is headed theoretically continues for some two hundred pages via a grueling, minutely documented compilation of the ways in which we in the West are killing ourselves—not needing terrorism in the slightest to bring the consequences of globalization home. With an archival skill that I never knew she had, and the collective skill of her research assistants no doubt, Teresa documents the slow death of our biosphere as a result of the process she has theorized up to now. She documents first the bad news most of us already know: the pollution of our air and creation of unstable climates through global warming (mainly through the deregulation of fossil fuels), the increase in our exposure to UV radiation, our unsafe water and toxic food supply—all of this speeded up exponentially by the increased ease of movement across old, state borders through new trans-corporate initiatives such as the most familiar NAFTA or GATT. She demonstrates once again how these initiatives have led *directly* to cuts in health care, pensions, education and more—with the inevitable global feminization of poverty so obvious to anyone who pays attention. (As Teresa points out, of the 1.3 billion people living on one U.S. dollar or less daily, one billion are women.)

But Teresa doesn't stop there. Like all good feminists, she brings us back, over and over again to our bodies. She digs up the statistics in this, her "empirical book": Chronic illness is now the central health issue of the advanced Western world. In the U.S. alone, 96% of home care visits, 83% of prescription drug use, 66% of physician visits and 55% of emergency department visits are for epidemic chronic conditions. Auto-immune diseases are increasing. Cancer and other chronic illnesses are escalating. One has less money as well as less time to repair the damage of staying in the race.

What can we do about this situation? It is not clear to me that we can do anything. But, Teresa is an incorrigible optimist because of her spiritual convictions and the ways in which they inflect her political beliefs. She acknowledges that today's world is at war. The economic war on the South by the North is going global and military, she says, and the "South" has engaged in return. She describes compellingly what she sees as two large, universalist ideologies, both appropriate to expansion, both ultimately fed by capital, both reviling liberated women and uncloseted homosexuals (i.e., those not willing to play the Foundational Fantasy Game), both claiming that the Judgment is at hand; the Apocalypse is now.

> [A]t a certain cumulative point, fossil fuel emissions really will destroy the life of the future. As they do so, aided by other aspects of Western capitalism, they bring into being the blood-red moon, the boiling seas littered with dead fish, the plagues, famine, and drought, the people who have to pay for water: all listed in the apocalyptic events of the Book of Revelation. Global

warming, the thing responsible, is mentioned as marking the end-time in Judaism's *Ein Yaakov,* insofar as it warns of great heat. To read Revelation and similar texts as visions of this future, here and soon, is to begin moving prophecy from the sphere of the inexplicable. As Freud noted, there are visions of probable futures in dreams and involuntary conscious images. Einstein added that everyday life in space and time is in some ways a fantasy. Freud attempted to find a rational line of cause and effect in accounting for premonitions and was unsuccessful. But that does not mean these things lie forever beyond human ken, anymore than the cause and effect leading to environmental disaster is beyond the reasoning of those prepared to read. The coincidence of the Protocol and the texts of apocalypse exists, I suggest, because reason is godlike and because God also works by reason and in fact is reason, even though much of this reason has remained beyond the comprehension of human creatures . . .

By following its deductive chain, by reaching the conclusion that the environmental disasters prophesied in various religions are our own work, this book seeks to persuade those whose reason led them [away] from faith that the metaphysical issues of religion are in fact issues for the here and now, and that the coincidence between the prophesies of the religions of the Book (and the West) and the realities of climate change is great enough to require an explanation. This argument also seeks to persuade those whose faith leads them to acts of suicide that they are perpetuating and expanding negative emotions and affects (fear, anger, the anxiety and pain which interfere with thinking) of which they are also victims. But it has begun by drawing attention to the coincidence between the prophesies of Kyoto and those of Revelation, prophesies which are common, with different stresses, to the three religions of the Book. I take the coincidence of human-made catastrophe and revelation as indicative of the way that humans are invested with more decision-making power than customary models of religion allow. If human beings have this much agency in shaping their fate, we should assume that the deadlines we set ourselves for reversing course are judgments whose day has indeed been determined—by ourselves. (Brennan 2003, xix-xxi)

Teresa argues that we—all of us North, South, East, and West of whatever faith, gender, class, color, or sex—must stop and *go back* out of a desire to keep living. We should be guided in going back, not by nostalgia, but by what Teresa called—not joking at all—The Prime Directive:

> The prime directive: we shall not use up nature and humankind at a rate faster than they can replenish themselves and be replenished . . . if we live by reason rather than faith, this is the inevitable conclusion. If we live by faith, we might reasonably recognize that the only judgment inflicted upon us is our own. (Brennan 2003, 164)

[margin handwritten note: Desire to keep living]

The Transmission of Affect

I don't know about you, but for me, it's really hard to know what to do and where to start, with such a huge directive, especially from beyond the grave. It is clear to me that, characteristically, Teresa decided to go back to the beginnings of her theory—to the Foundational Fantasy, to the Western Social Psychosis, to her theory of energetics and what she sees as the death-driven exploitation of energy today, that of the earth, of entire human groups and individuals. She decided to go back to the ego, to disconnect it and its subject/object paradigm increasingly in control of the planet. Thus, in the fifth instance, we have *The Transmission of Affect* (2004). This was the book she was working on just before being hit by a speeding, out of control, and still unaccounted for car.

I am not going to spend a lot of time on this fifth volume, in part because this book, strangely unfinished, was clearly her first best effort to answer her favorite question, "What is to be done?" in accord with the Prime Directive. For Teresa, the first thing we have to do is prove the relativity of the Imperial Ego and work toward a realignment of its functions more in accord with the goal of protecting life than spreading death. Above all, we must educate, argue and act, with those we love as well as with those we hate (or who hate us), to begin to cut the juice, to starve the logic of total war. Uncharacteristically, but ambitiously, Teresa turns to science—biology, chemistry and physics—and especially to neuroscience and endocrinology, to prove that the transmission of affect is all around us in the North, South, East, and, yes, even the West if we are willing and able to discern it. The social enters the biological. That is "the new paradigm" she represents to us:

> What is at stake with the notion of the transmission of affect is precisely the opposite of the sociobiological claim that the biological *determines* the social. What is at stake is rather the means by which social interaction shapes biology. My affect, if it comes across to you, alters your anatomical makeup for good or ill. (Brennan 2004, 74)

From the "entrainment" of hormonal, electrical, magnetic connections ordering everything from group psychology to "interpersonal depression" or ADHD as disorders of attentive energy, Teresa passionately but rationally argues for a new education of the senses and "a lifting of the burden of the ego" so that the social psychosis currently in charge of the world's fate can be decoded and undone.

Just before her voice went silent, Teresa implored us to give language to that which works toward life, to not be afraid or intimidated or self-censoring in our efforts to speak for life and put a stop to the increase in death all around us today. I give her her own last words:

If it yet seems that with the resurrection of the body, I have resurrected the specter of demons to be struggled against and overthrown, this is also true. But once it is recognized that these demons are familiar affective patterns that can be undone, that these affects can be countered whenever we refuse them entry, once, in short, that they are understood as forces in human affairs that can be cleaned up and transformed, converted back into living energy as they are released from distorting blocks of inertia and repression, then they have no power to whip up the superstition, anger, and anxiety that prevail when their capabilities are inflated. They have power only when we see them, hear them, think them, as well as smell and touch and taste them—and then grant them admission. Their power to torment us exists only as long as we permit it to exist. It is our living energy these demons thrive on, and it is only theirs when diverted through ignorance from the drive to love and create into the pathways of war, exploitation, and death. Of that we cannot speak, thereof we must learn. (Brennan 2004, 163–164)

References

Brennan, Teresa. 2004. *The Transmission of Affect*. Ithaca: Cornell University Press.

———2003. *Globalization and its Terrors: Daily Life in the West*. London: Routledge.

———2000. *Exhausting Modernity: Grounds for a New Economy*. London: Routledge.

———1993. *History After Lacan*. London: Routledge.

———1992. *The Interpretation of the Flesh: Freud and Femininity*. London: Routledge.

CHAPTER TWO

Living A Tension

⸺⚬❦⚬⸺

Kelly Oliver

*T*ERESA WAS HOSTING CHRISTMAS DINNER *at her apartment in New York City, inviting a few of her eclectic friends. I was staying with her for a few weeks while we wrote the introduction and proposal for a book that she was convinced we would write together on affect, energy and, as always, maternity. It was 1995. I had met Teresa several years earlier at a conference and had visited her in Cambridge and she visited me in Austin.*

On this sparkling December afternoon, she was planning a traditional Christmas dinner with turkey, stuffing, and sweet potatoes. But as we started to cook, it came as a shock to me that she had no roasting pan or mixing bowls, and barely any ingredients for the feast that she imagined. Yet, somehow, almost through sheer imagination and will, we made a dinner that was not only satisfying but also tasty.

I remember other times later when Teresa invited me to Florida to continue our collaboration and, when in a similar spirit, taking this and that from here and there, and mixing together an unlikely combination of whatever we could find, we made a dreadful mess and ended up ordering pizza.

Before we went to midnight mass at St. Patrick's Cathedral, Teresa's friend Joni, the psychic, read tarot cards to predict the success of our collaboration. Like any good psychic, she was non-committal. The saints at St. Patrick's had even less to say about our future success than Joni. But the pure joy of singing hymns together proved the theory of the circulation of energy and the transmission of affect. Teresa used to say that we were going to be the "Horkheimer and Adorno" of a new "school" of affect. I approached her grand visions much like I did her fantasies of the feast that we prepared out of the meager stale leftovers in her refrigerator. For me, her life and thought seemed bold, risky, intimidating and compelling.

With risks come possibilities for creativity and imagination—a creative force that takes bits and pieces from here and there and mixes them together into a powerful stimulant if not elixir. In Brennan's work, we risk losing

13

boundaries—disciplinary boundaries, the boundaries of the self, of drives and affects, of the academy. Paradoxically, however, her texts also seem to be mobilized by dichotomies of good and evil that set up oppositions between bound versus free, slow versus fast, artificial versus natural, imitation versus original, distant versus close, self-containment versus mobility, health versus illness, and even, in the end, the devil versus god. But, the boundaries between these pairs are also blurred and it is not always clear which of the two is good and which is evil. In spite of these shifting valuations throughout her work, especially in her latest work, there is very little discussion of ethics. For Brennan, discussions of good and evil are framed by religion, particularly Christianity.

Containment Versus Mobility

In her first two books, Brennan maintains that self-containment is an illusion fed by hallucinations and fantasies that keep us in a destructive cycle of denial and abuse. In *The Interpretation of the Flesh* (1992), she argues that those who occupy the feminine position give loving living attention to others but do not receive it themselves. This living attention shores up and supports the ego. If attention does not come from the outside, then it must be produced from inside. But this process of self-attending is not effective because the energy required to construct the fantasies used to support one's own ego exceeds the energy produced by them. Those in the feminine position are left with unproductive daydreaming causing delays in real achievements by substituting them with fantasies. In these feminine fantasies, drive energy turns inward, which is a type of containment of energy that Brennan suggests is unhealthy. Drive energy is healthy when it is free to circulate and not bound or contained within one ego.

The notion that psychic energy circulates between people is one of the most revolutionary notions in Brennan's early work. Even drives are not self-contained within one psyche. Brennan calls the illusion that we are self-contained the "foundational fantasy," which she describes in *History After Lacan* (1993) as based on the primal hallucination that the infant controls the mother's breast. But the foundational fantasy comes at the price of sacrificing the original/maternal/earth for an imitation/hallucination, which leads to the destruction and abuse of the original/maternal/earth upon which the ego depends and therefore ultimately leads to self-destruction. The foundational fantasy is an attempt to contain psychic energy and fix it in order to control it: "hallucination makes us self-contained because it divorces mindful agency from the matter that executes it—matter it makes passive in fantasy—and because hallucination situates the subject in a fixed place, from which it functions at a slower pace, in energetic terms" (Brennan 1993, 67).

The foundational fantasy slows down the circulation of energy, fixes it, and thereby stagnates the very life forces that sustain the body and psyche. The life force of the original/maternal/earth is imagined as passive in order to reassure the subject of his own agency and activity, which in turn legitimates his use and abuse of that passive matter. The connection between the foundational fantasy and the exploitation and destruction of the environment is made explicit in *Exhausting Modernity* (2000) and *Globalization and its Terrors* (2003). In these later works, Brennan links the foundational fantasy and the political economy of global capitalism. But this move from the psyche to the economic, from the personal to the political, from the individual to the social, also leads to an ambivalent valuation of self-containment and mobility. Whereas at the personal level of the individual psyche, self-containment is hallucination, perhaps a necessary evil, that leads to destruction of the environment, on the economic level self-containment may be the only antidote to the destructive forces of globalization on the environment and on peoples of the regions exploited far from the beneficiaries' own backyards.

Brennan argues that we need a "new protectionism" to "reverse the concentration of wealth on the one hand, and the distance over which natural resources can be obtained on the other" (Brennan 2003, 156). She maintains that "the closer to home one's energy sources and raw materials are, the more one's reproduction costs stay in line; paid and domestic labor will be less exploited, and the environment less depleted" (ibid., 160). This leads her to an appeal for "economic self-containment," which she suggests will facilitate other more creative forms of cultural exchange. While economic exchange should be limited and self-contained, intellectual exchange should be promoted. Brennan concludes that once economic self-containment is in effect, "there is more healthy or good fruit, more diversity of fruit, and that fruit is closer to home" (ibid., 171). I wonder if self-contained local economies would or could encourage and produce diversity. It seems that the contact with people across the globe that comes with the global economy has exposed us to diversity, even if it is always in a sense "prepackaged."

For Brennan, economic self-containment on a global scale is good whereas at the personal level self-containment is a destructive illusion, especially in the form of feminine fantasy and daydreaming that limit productivity. She suggests that personal productivity should be expanded and mobile while economic productivity should be limited and self-contained. In fact, given Brennan's arguments about the exhaustion that comes with global capitalism, it seems that personal and economic energy are inversely correlated such that limitations on global economy will lead to mobilization of personal energy.

Brennan's last book, *The Transmission of Affect* (2004), moves back from the global to the personal or psychic level, only now prescribing affective self-containment on the individual level as a protection against what she calls "negative affects." She describes two types of self-containment, projection (destructive and delusional self-containment) and discernment (healthy self-containment):

> . . . the resister in the group and the clinician who discerns have in common an ability to distance or detach. But this mysterious ability, this aptly called 'self-possession,' may come into focus more clearly if we consider what it is not . . . Projecting is the opposite of discernment because projection directs affects outward without consciously (as a rule) acknowledging that it is doing so; discernment consciously examines them. Boundaries may depend on projecting, but this is only one route to self-containment. There is another, based on discernment. (Brennan 2004, 11)

In terms of (negative) affect, as in the case of uncontained global economies, we need a "new protectionism" that works toward containment and limits mobility and exchange. But whereas Brennan counsels closeness in terms of economies of capital, she recommends distance and detachment in relation to economies of affects. Discernment requires the distance and detachment of reflection, which can protect against harmful negative affects coming from outside through the realization that they do not originate in the self. This process leads to the self-containment of negative affects, which relieves the subject from the need to carry the burden of the affects of others. In her last book, Brennan provides a therapy for the symptoms of femininity that she diagnosed in her first book. Those in the feminine position, or what she refers to as "the dumpees," must learn to discern which affects are their own and which are "dumped" on them by others and then they must bar the offending affects from entering their psyches.

Brennan's analysis suggests that negative affects come from the outside while only positive ones come from the inside. This distinction between inside and outside seems to work against the underlying insight of both her first and last books: that affective and drive energy is not self-contained but circulates. Her theory of the transmission of affect and circulation of drive energy begins to read more like a warning against the dangers of the circulation of affect against which so much philosophy protects itself by virtue of projection and the foundational fantasy. Indeed, the foundational fantasy seems justified given the dangers of the transmission of affect, which are demonized in Brennan's last work:

> They [negative affects] have power only when we see them, hear them, think them, as well as smell and touch and taste them—and then grant them admission. Their power to torment us exists only as long as we permit it to exist. It is our living energy these demons thrive on, and it is only theirs when diverted through ignorance from the drive to love and create

into the pathways of conquest, war, exploitation, and death. Of that we cannot speak, thereof we must learn. (Brennan 2004, 164)

Yet, for Brennan, the foundational fantasy is also one of the ways through
which living energy is diverted from creativity and love to conquest and war.
Feminine fantasy is another such destructive diversion. And the projection
of negative affects onto others is a result of the foundational fantasy and the
affective division of labor that makes those in the masculine position "dump-
ers" and those in the feminine position "dumpees." Moreover, Brennan's
solution also seems to rely on the foundational fantasy that we can be self-
contained individuals. Her concept of discernment turns the foundational
fantasy against itself and uses the illusions of autonomy and self-control to
fight the negative effects of diverting living energy into the service of those
very illusions.

The conclusions of both her first and last book read as calls to individuals
to take control of their psychic and affective lives and reclaim their own good,
positive, creative, living energy against the forces of evil, negative, destructive, deadly forces. The conclusion to the *Transmission of Affect* quoted above
makes it clear that it is up to individuals to deny access to the demons of negative affects (which Brennan also links to the seven deadly sins): because our
torment comes from "demons" outside ourselves, we can protect against them
by shutting them out. The conclusion to *The Transmission of Affect* echoes the
conclusion to *The Interpretation of the Flesh* in which Brennan calls on those
in the feminine position to quit daydreaming and do something by choosing
to deny power to the death drive and its delays:

> A woman, or any feminine being, can reclaim her heritage, and sever her tie
> to the past. All that stands in the way of her doing so is an identity by which
> she is protected, but which nonetheless slows her down. It slows her down
> because of the death drive it contains. Yet, the power of the death drive is
> only time, whose power in turn is naught but the delay between the concep-
> tion of an idea, and its execution. (Brennan 1992, 240)

She seems to conclude that if we suffer it is because we have been forced to
carry affects that are not our own—which also assumes that our own affects
are not negative or deadly; and if we have been forced to carry the affective
burdens of others, then we should simply stop doing so.

This call to individuals to sever the past, stop day-dreaming and start
acting, or to stop permitting demon affects from entering our psyches, could
be Brennan's way of reclaiming agency for the "dumpees" who occupy the
feminine or exploited position. Yet, without formulating resistance strategies, her call to action requires a large dose of stoicism that may be difficult
for those othered within patriarchal global economies. Moreover, although

it appears that Brennan's attribution of responsibility and thereby agency to those oppressed by negative affects brings with it an ethical responsibility to be true to oneself, it falls short of an ethical demand for self-critical hermeneutics that interrogates the ways in which we are not only complicit with the circulation of negative affects and global exploitation but also the ways in which we generate and profit from those demons.

In her last book, it seems that our only ethical responsibility is to a form of absolute repression that excludes the negative affects of anger, depression, greed, etc. from our own psychic space—an absolute repression of the death drive. But, as Freud teaches us, the more absolute and violent the repression, the more absolute and violent the return of the repressed.

Slow versus Fast

If at the conclusion to *The Interpretation of the Flesh* Brennan tells us to sever our tie to the past and fight against that which slows us down, in *Globalization and its Terrors* she tells us to "go back, slow down" (Brennan 2003, 165). Perhaps this suggests that there is a middle ground, a just right pace, between too slow or delayed and too fast or speedy, between the past of feminine underachievement and the future of masculine globalization. In both cases, she suggests that we need to stop what she sees as the drive to death if not the death drive; indeed we will be "judged" if we don't (ibid.,167). In her later work, Brennan proposes that the principle that we use to go back is what she calls (borrowing from the television show Star Trek) "the prime directive": "we shall not use up nature and humankind at a rate faster than they can replenish themselves or be replenished" (ibid., 164). The prime directive could also be applied to the living attention that Brennan analyzes in *The Interpretation of the Flesh*, in which case it would read something like this: We shall not use energy or living attention at a rate faster than they can replenish themselves or be replenished. Both the masculine foundational fantasy sustained by the living attention of others and feminine fantasy or day-dreaming use more energy than they produce; they appear to provide instant gratification but in reality they slow down satisfaction and achievement.

In addition, Brennan endorses biodegradability as a way to distinguish healthy from unhealthy time. Fast re-entry into the life cycle through biodegradation helps regenerate and replenish the earth. Pollutants that result from global capital do not re-enter the life cycle fast enough and therefore damage the environment and break the prime directive. From *History After Lacan* through *Globalization and its Terrors*, Brennan argues that global capitalism speeds up time and appears to go faster by creating an artificial time of production that is at odds with the natural time of reproduction: "The construction of more and more commodities slows down real time while seeming to speed it up" (Brennan 1993, 183) "This 'slower movement' which is key to the exhausting nature of modernity . . . underpins a different sense of time, one that appears fast, but is in fact slower, than that of life" (Brennan 2000, 68–9).

The production and delivery of goods and services appears to get faster but in reality the time of reproduction slows down as the natural resources necessary for production are not renewed or regenerated. Brennan identifies these "two forms of time" as "the generational time of natural reproduction, and speed, the artificial time of the short-term profit" (ibid., 126). She warns that natural energy is being depleted and otherwise converted into artificial energies that, like feminine daydreaming, actually in the long run consume more energy than they produce (cf. ibid., 105). This process of exhaustion produces the artificial sense of time and energy opposed to, and covering over, the natural generational time and energy of reproduction.

Brennan also makes a distinction between fast and speedy. Some forms of fast are good, while others, most particularly speedy ones, are bad or unhealthy. This distinction is made most explicitly in one of the many apocalyptic moments where she appeals to religion, specifically Christianity, in *Globalization and its Terrors*:

> If God allows us liberty in this respect (human free will), surely we have it in relation to setting our own deadlines (the first rule of good pedagogy)—a matter again of good judgment . . . If the followers of all religions were to feel themselves bound by the prime directive in the transactions of everyday life, this would generate the kind of spiritual force that underpins all justified revolutions, and do so fast enough to enable us to reverse course in time, which at least means honoring our own deadlines. Being fast to the right end is not the same as being speedy. Being fast is the result of a clear head and clear direction, without the need for escape time generated by physical and mental depression. (Brennan 2003, 167)

Brennan urges us to be fast in going back by avoiding speed with a clear resolve that comes from the righteousness of a "justified revolution." Yet, this clear head and direction that require no reflection and lead to doing rather than escapist daydreaming seems again at odds with the distance and mediation necessary for discernment in the realm of affects. In discussing time and speed in relation to affect, it becomes less certain for Brennan which is better—going fast or going slow. Jane Gallop points to this tension when in her analysis of *The Transmission of Affect* she notes, "While Brennan may privilege faster over slow, she nonetheless does not like 'rushed'" (this volume, p. 113). Discernment requires mediation and distance and slows down the fast action of the affects themselves; but it does not engage in the delay tactics used by the ego with its hallucinations and projections that substitute the imitation for the original (which resonates with global capital's substitution of the artificial for the real). Rather, what is discerned through this deliberate reflection on affects is precisely their external origin, and thereby one's own "real" affects versus "artificial" affects that come from outside.

As in her analysis of global capital, here too in terms of affects, Brennan prefers the natural to the artificial or constructed. Flying in the face of discourse analysis and deconstructions of the origin/imitation and immediate/mediated binaries, not to mention feminist criticisms of the natural/constructed (nature/culture) dichotomy, Brennan insists on the value of the real or natural over the fantasy or artificial because constructions, whether they are fantasies or interpretations, slow us down:

> Just as the subject overlays the (retroactively) faster world of chemical and hormonal communication—in which it first stored memories—with the slower world contingent on seeing things from its own stand-point, so too does he lose the means for rapid interpretation of the logics of the flesh . . . The subject-to-be loses touch with the pathways that connect him without impediment when he has to pause in the face of an image and learn to ask whether the image is real or illusory . . . The energy that escapes service in the name of fixation is misdirected in the affected drives: It is directed away from the living paths it otherwise follows naturally toward the constructed pathways of subjectivity, pathways built around inertia and lack. (Brennan 2004, 148)

Brennan's recommendation is again to go back this time to "reconnect language and understanding with the fleshly and environmental codes from which our consciousness has been split by fantasy and illusion" (ibid., 148–9). The "correct alignment" of linguistic and bodily codes leads to an "unimpeded for less-impeded flow of energy," which in turn makes us quicker (ibid., 149). She maintains that our thinking and responses are faster, even speedier, when the word and the flesh are made one through proper alignment and when linguistic constructions are in tune with the body's "intelligence," therefore leading to direct communication and action. In terms of her analysis of affects, then, even speed is good because the body is fast and thought is quick when it comes directly from the body (that is to say one's *own* body and not the bodies of others). To be *rushed,* on the other hand, makes sense only in the constructed artificial time because nature is never rushed even when it is fast and obtains its own "force and speed" (ibid., 146).

The body, it seems, provides instant knowledge and gratification whereas the ego only distorts its natural origins through hallucinations and fantasies of knowledge and gratification that destroy the very body from which they originate. Given that we live in what Brennan calls the era of the ego, all we can hope for is the wherewithal to discern the real from the illusory, the natural from the man-made, reproduction from production, and act deliberately on that discernment "to go back." Yet, if, as Brennan suggests, the "physical reality in which we exist, the physical laws under which we live, are being and have been altered" (Brennan 1993, 183), then how can we distinguish between the natural and the artificial? And, given the ego's effectiveness in deception, how can we be sure that we know, or that we are on the side of righteousness, even after our self-reflection? Isn't Brennan's own vision of going back to nature by following the prime directive a fantasy of greener grass that she explicitly rejects (cf. Brennan 2004, 14, 153)? Indeed, don't we need fantasy to imagine alternative futures and better realities? Finally, how do we reconcile Brennan's valuation of a fast reentry into the life cycle through biodegradability (eg., Brennan 1993, 176) and her reluctance to accept that negative affects are part of that cycle, especially if, as she claims, they lead to faster aging and decay, that is, faster reentry into the life cycle (Brennan 2004, 151)?

Brennan's notion of the circulation of energy and transmission of affect give us the theoretical tools to develop an ethics and politics of difference with a radical responsibility for others and the environment; although this ethics remains underdeveloped in her work. It is not the ability to discern the difference between real or original from artificial or imitation (whether we are talking about affects, mothers, or the earth) that serves life. Rather, discernment serves life when it enables us to continually interpret and reinterpret our fantasies, when it turns the foundational fantasy back on itself and makes us suspicious of our own desires. Self-reflection slows us down, but it also makes us more deliberate and responsible. Brennan's urgent appeals to slow down the economy of global capital must also be applied to the economy of affects. The fact that reflection and analysis slows us down could be one reason why our speed driven culture prefers the unselfconscious reactions of *Forrest Gump* or *Dumb and Dumber* to sustained self-reflection. Thinking is not efficient and ultimately leads to infinite questioning and self-interrogation that slows down both the economy of global capitalism and the economy of affect.

Perhaps the foundational fantasy's slowing mechanism is also a protective mechanism against self-destruction. But interpretation and self-reflection work in the service of life only when they become the ethical decision, made over and over again, to take responsibility not only for one's fantasies of greener-grass but also for one's own negative affects and their effects on others. Learning to protect ourselves from the negative affects of others, especially those cultivated by our culture, may be necessary for happiness or peace of mind. But only when this discernment is combined with taking responsibility for our own complicity with, and generation of, those destructive negative affects that lead to greed and war can we hope for an ethics and politics of difference that might help us mitigate against the effects of global capital and the affective exploitation and colonization of those othered.

Beyond Brennan's analysis, we not only need to take responsibility for negative affects but also acknowledge the positive effects of the transmission of affect in relationships that create a surplus of living attention and energy. Profit and surplus in terms of capital may be exploitative but the group dynamics that Brennan discusses in *The Transmission of Affect* make it clear that we can get more than we put in, that the whole is larger than the sum of its parts, when it comes to people working or playing together. Indeed, rather than talk of devils and gods, it seems to me that we encounter something transcendent or divine in our interactions with others and our environment. It is what is between us that puts us in touch with something beyond the ego. In fact, after Brennan's deconstruction of the ego and its foundational fantasy, perhaps one way to imagine renewed agency is a result of the circulation of energy between and among people. The circulation of energy and transmission of affect make it possible to think of agency that comes not from an individual ego or consciousness, but rather from shared experiences and group dynamics (no matter how small the group).

Teresa knew this in her own life. She always surrounded herself with would-be collaborators, especially smart women, in the hopes that together they could cook up something greater than any one of them could individually. It is difficult to envision the possibility of creating something good and nourishing from the leftovers of patriarchy and global capital without working together taking this and that from here and there and using whatever is available along with a large measure of collective imagination and innovation.

References

Brennan, Teresa. 2004. *The Transmission of Affect*. Ithaca: Cornell University Press.

———2003. *Globalization and its Terrors: Daily Life in the West*. London: Routledge.

———2000. *Exhausting Modernity: Grounds for a New Economy*. London: Routledge.

———1993. *History After Lacan*. London: Routledge.

———1992. *The Interpretation of the Flesh: Freud and Femininity*. London: Routledge.

CHAPTER THREE

Time Difference

The Political Psychoanalysis of Teresa Brennan

———— ❧❧❧ ————

Robyn Ferrell

TERESA BRENNAN WROTE, as maybe all do at the moment of creation, in a time zone between conviction and madness, ignominy and brilliance. Above all, she wrote in pursuit of a platform on which to put up her leftist political conviction alongside her feminist outrage and her psychoanalytic understanding of affective life.

In order to render my admiration for her writing, I want to take up the figure of the time difference in relation to Teresa Brennan's life and work while I also express my ambivalence about her conclusions. By "time difference," I mean the sense of the difference between then and now, the difference between Australia and the US, and the difference between her and me. I also mean the difference that time *makes*, in terms of what is possible then—for example, when *History After Lacan* was first published in 1993, the year I met Teresa—and now. In terms of how one reads the work then and now, is it more or less convincing now? Was she ahead of her time, or just outside it, in another time zone? How do texts move between time zones?

Among other things this paper will explore the infinitesimal difference between being Australian and being American or being English; to ask what, in this time of globalization, does a 14-hour time difference amount to? To do this is to take up the geopolitics of philosophy, something central in Teresa Brennan's work. In *History After Lacan* and other works, she developed a kind of political psychoanalysis that directly engaged globalization in a novel way, as a subject-formation in which the real and the psychical are caught in a "feedback loop."

The geo-politics of philosophy was also something Teresa's *life* represented to me. When I met her she was an Australian working "overseas," successful in academic theaters like Cambridge and New York. These places were so far from "home" in Melbourne and Sydney, they became the object of the Australian academic subject's fantasied projections. This paper is partly about those projections, which are naturally my own.

Teresa was not trained as a philosopher, and so my argument—that *her* argument addresses Australian materialism, at least as much as its explicit intellectual context—is fanciful in "real time." Not only that, but my reading is partial in two senses, in that it can only address an aspect of Teresa's work and also that it represent the "views of the author," views not necessarily in agreement with Teresa's own.

But I don't suppose this is anything to be surprised at, much less disturbed by. Teresa and I had this in common. That we come from a time zone where the similarity between philosophy and a fist fight has always been closer than they are in New York; from a zone of the academy where the proximity between a fist fight and a pub brawl were many times inevitable.

One of the things that most struck me, when I turned again to read *History After Lacan,* was how there is in Teresa's style something argumentative and didactic, a dogmatic, or at least high-handed exercise, like someone shouting something. I suggest that what she was shouting was: "It *does* make sense! I'm *not* mad!"

Many readers of *History After Lacan* will have gathered she is attempting to construct an ontological link between Marxism and psychoanalysis. Fewer readers may have read in it an attempt to defend a theory of "mind-brain identity," perhaps only this one idiosyncratic reader. But, despite my education in Australian materialism, I never did *get it*. The propositions of analytic philosophy attacked me like a corrosive substance to which I was allergic. The philosophical methods of this genre were wrung out of me at the expense of any intellectual vivacity I had. I would have given up on philosophy if I hadn't come into contact with highly addictive substances in psychoanalytic theory and deconstruction. Reading Freud, Lacan, and Derrida helped me, as reading Freud, Lacan, and Marx obviously helped Teresa, to make sense of a reasonable madness.

The difference between then and now, that is, between doing theoretical work in Australia in the seventies and now, is a difference of time. Thirty years of shouting, "We're not mad" has actually had an effect. In my own field of feminist philosophy, the work of Elizabeth Grosz, Genevieve Lloyd, Moira Gatens, Carole Pateman, Rosi Braidotti, Ros Diprose, Pene Deutscher, and others have created a space, or perhaps a time, for feminist philosophy, as has the scholarship in phenomenology and existential philosophy of Paul Patton, George Marcus, Kevin Hart, Max Deutscher, Andrew Benjamin, Brian Massumi, to name a few. Although the features that bring my work close to Teresa's—a central role for psychoanalysis, for feminist theory and for

"European" philosophical approaches—are not those in which that style of philosophy known as "Australian materialism" is couched, it has been nevertheless through that machismo, pugilist, and reductive strain of thought that I have found the most compelling insight into Teresa's project.

The way I read *History After Lacan*, it argues with David Armstrong, Jack Smart, and the other Australian materialists, in a language far from any they would find common-sensical or even comprehensible, and from a theoretical synthesis of Marxism and Lacanian psychoanalysis that would have struck them as preposterous, not because of the audacity of its intellectual ambition, but because Marx was a communist and Lacan was a foreigner.

To my knowledge, Teresa didn't study, or study with, these figures. Yet the philosophy of Australian materialism distils most pungently the empiricism-cum-anti-intellectualism that has traditionally governed Australian scholarship. I can't help but imagine her book as an argument against all those belligerent philosophers who held that there was no other world but the physical.

This is a difference in time and place that is obscured by the supposedly international forum of philosophical work. Or better, it refers to a *geophilosophy* such as Derrida writes of, in "The Ends of Man" (1978), warning us against the seductive syllable "we" in the conduct of metaphysics. Who is "we," he asks Heidegger, such that we might generalize about our being? Is there such a thing as the "*Australian* philosopher," or is regionalism not a quality pertaining to philosophy, and if there were, could he be a *she* (or is sexual difference an ontological difference)?

To use another paradigm, in Deleuze and Guattari's view of philosophy,[1] concepts arise on geopolitical planes that support them, different in different times and places, scratching a different itch. But the concept arises always in relation to the philosophical persona that it addresses; if the Australian materialist is one's interlocutor, is this persona ever feminine? I think the answer is no; and I think, not only as a polemicist, but as a reader of the philosophy of technology, where, as Teresa attempts to capture in the thesis below, the subject is inevitably masculine.

My discussion is ordered by Brennan's own "theses," presented at the beginning of *History After Lacan* and condensing her theoretical ambitions for it.

> *Thesis 1: The subject is founded by a hallucinatory fantasy in which it conceives itself as the locus of active agency and the environment as passive; its subjectivity is secured by a projection onto the environment, apparently beginning with the mother, which makes her into an object which the subject in fantasy controls.*
> (Brennan 1993, 11)

While Brennan draws her inspiration from Lacan in many of her propositions in the book, her notion of the subject owes more to object-relations theory. It can perhaps be seen in this how Lacan has functioned as an inspiration more in the way that one speaks of the male artist and the muse. It is also likely that Lacan functions, as she gestures toward at one point, as the very fixed point of a theory designed to unmask fixed points.

> In *The Interpretation of Flesh*, I wrote that the ego depends on fixed points because it depends on its identifications with others, and ideas, to maintain its sense of its individual distinctness, or identity . . . In this book I argue that the fixed points of the psyche are parallelled and reinforced by the construction of commodities in the social world . . . (Brennan 1993, xii)

This leads her to present an extreme identification of psychical and material life, which governs her later argument:

> In an interactive understanding of energy, the barriers that we erect between thought and matter, individual and environment, are precisely socially constructed ones. What happens on the socially constructed outside has energetic consequences for the psyche. (ibid.)

Her argument then proceeds in the *other* direction; that is, the psyche first constructs the social construction, or at least the rhetoric invokes the psychical terms to describe the social before discovering itself again in those terms. She writes, " . . . the history of modernity is the *acting out of a fantasy* and a *psychosis* by a technology and economy in which fixed points proliferate etc." (Brennan 1993, xii). She addresses this point, anticipating criticism, with a postulation of transmutable energy between psyches. She answers it by reversing the criticism, asking how it is that we come to experience ourselves as contained, in terms of our energies and affects. She concludes it is a prejudice of modernity that we experience ourselves as contained in that we are physically connected through a kind of subject-substance that is "literally in the air" (ibid., 10). However counter-intuitive it may seem, our real element would be the reductive one, and it is our experience of ourselves *as ego* that leads us to be mistaken about this nature of things.

Is the circularity of these formulations of psychical and social a fault in the argument, or an accurate observation of a zone? To answer this point, I will introduce below the converse circularity, brought out in this other kind of materialism that I am reminded of by Brennan's thought.

> *Thesis 2: The foundational fantasy is the basis of the subject's conceiving itself as contained in energetic terms. To the extent that the fantasy dominates the subject's psyche, knowledge or experience of energetic connections between beings and entities is foreclosed.* (Brennan 1993, 12)

This is the point at which I start to think of Australian philosopher Jack Smart, and his "identity theory of mind."

In the sixties, Jack Smart argued for a kind of physicalism asserting that reports of inner mental states were best understood as referring to brain states, even if the possessor of these mental states did not know this (Presley, 1971). This was a philosophical ruse for dispensing with a dualism that was cluttering up the landscape of scientific realism. It had the merit of going to meet the alarming advance of the biotechnological, but it did this literally at the expense of other sensibilities. Later (1988), in response to what he thought of, no doubt, as the *threat* of relativism, Smart declared, "After all, there are some *things*. There are chaps, and chairs . . ." [2]

It is not in any straightforward sense that I hear the echo of Australian materialism in Brennan's formulations. It is more in the manner of speaking literally . . . On one level, Brennan is asserting the very opposite of mind-brain identity. In her vision, those things which are real are created so by the action of my thought, whereas in Smart's case those thoughts are real by cause of the action of various "things" like electrochemical events etc. So hers is more properly a kind of "brain-mind identity."

In another sense, the notions are identically reductive, and similarly implausible. Max Deutscher conceded the dilemma, in his consideration of Smart's theory:

> If someone's being struck by a thought is not an event in any particular part of his body, nor a general state of his body, nor an event involving all of his body, then how in the name of philosophy are we to think of its being located where the body is? . . . The feeling is that we know without any sort of argument or inference that physicalism is false. For one thing we know this by our immediate acquaintance with the richness of our sensory experience. However, when I try to catch this feeling by the throat and make it speak, all I get are bad arguments. (Presley 1971, 78–79)

Bad arguments: This foregrounds the stake of rhetoric, which I will later develop. What this interesting inversion offers me, in terms of Brennan's own political vision, is an insight into a decided sexual dimorphism in Australian theory—a truculent philosophy of mind alongside an insistent philosophy of the body, and a "boys' own" objective account of (the) matter, while subjective accounts become "secret women's business."

> *Thesis 3: Before the advent of a Western technology capable of fulfilling the desires embodied in the foundational fantasy, it is contained. The advent of that technology is prompted by the fantasy and represents an acting out of it on an increasingly global scale, an enactment that reinforces the psychical power of the fantasy.* (Brennan 1993, 13)

The intriguing problem that Lacan brings forward is the essentially fantasmagorical nature of thought, including the "paranoic structure of knowledge."

This is not "curable" In Lacan's view, the best that can happen is that one becomes aware of the "sliding of signifiers" under the fixing of the ego. Lacan has been roundly criticised for the paradox of finding a pathology in the unavoidable condition of subjectivity.

Brennan blows this insight up large, so that now it truly counts as paranoid. Circularity is a feature of the psychotic, in as much as—and Brennan describes this—one's projections return to oneself as signs from "outside." The confusion of words and things, the formation of words *as* things and the transformation of matter into signs, is the central dilemma of empiricism.

Only Deleuze, Brennan says, criticizing other post-structuralists, can "entertain the idea that the subject is not self-contained at the material level of energy" (Brennan 1993, 11). This assumes that "energy" is a thing, whereas for Deleuze it remains a concept, even if that has a materiality. It brings to mind his critique of empiricism:

> Empiricism is by no means a reaction against concepts, nor a simple appeal to lived experience. On the contrary, it undertakes the most insane creation of concepts ever seen or heard. Empiricism treats the concept as object of an encounter, as a here-and-now . . . Only an empiricist could say: concepts are indeed things, but things in their free and wild state, beyond anthropological predicates. (Deleuze 1996, xx-xxi)

> *Thesis 4: The foundational fantasy is not fantasmatic because there are no foundations. It is fantasmatic because of the illusory foundations it structures and proceeds to make material, which overlie the natural generative foundation with which it competes.* (Brennan 1993, 16)

At this point, Brennan's reading parts company with Lacan. The only "natural" thing postulated in Lacan is "the effect in man of an organic insufficiency in his natural reality . . . This relation to nature is altered by a certain dehiscence at the heart of the organism, a primordial Discord . . ." (Lacan 1977, 4).

The "generative foundation" Brennan writes of does not have a place in Lacan's vision of the subject, strung as he sees it between its *points de capiton*. "The unconscious is neither primordial nor instinctual; what it knows about the elementary is no more than the elements of the signifier" (Lacan 1977, 170).

In place of a "natural generative foundation," Lacanian theory would postulate the Big "O" Other, returning to haunt the ego. Lacan writes : "The slightest alteration in the relation between man and the signifier . . . changes the whole course of history by modifying the moorings that anchor his being" (Lacan 1977, 174).[3]

With Thesis 4, we have left Lacanian psychoanalysis and entered into the maternal fantasies of object relations. Brennan's formulations offer a "generative foundation" but this assurance is refused by Lacan, through his postulation that there is a dehiscence of the subject which unsettles all foundation. The conviction of foundation would be a religious one in Lacan's thought—"God is not dead, he is Unconscious," as he says in *Four Fundamental Concepts*—and as such, knowledge of it would be a protective psychosis. Feminist psychoanalytic reflections may have led Brennan here through the notion of the maternal ground and especially its eclipse in the egocentric subject. Whatever else the merits of it, this commitment has given her, theoretically, a history after Lacan.

> *Thesis 5: The means by which time is compressed for space is identical to the process of producing profit. In this process, distance takes the place of the time of natural reproduction, for overall profit depends on binding natural substance and energy in commodities at a faster rate than nature can reproduce.* (Brennan 1993, 17)

In this thesis, a reduction is enacted in which time and space naturalize economy. The phrase "is identical to" elicits criticism from Anthony Easthope:

> The subject in ideology and the subject of the unconscious are distinct and cannot be theorized with a single totalising conception yet are always empirically related so that (to follow Saussure's metaphor . . .) a change in one cannot happen without a change in the other (you cannot cut the front of the paper without cutting the back). (Easthope 1995, 355)

The image of the recto and verso of the one piece of paper advances a critique of the same reduction of materialism as that in the Australian tradition. For example, U.T. Place, another Australian materialist, dealt with a logical objection to his reduction of the mind to the brain by addressing an analogous strategy. The examples he used were simple exercises in the copula: "*A square is an equilateral rectangle*" versus "*His table is a packing case*" (Place, 1956).

In *A History of Philosophy in Australia*, S.A. Grave comments:

> It is essentially *not* part of Place's theory that statements about sensations and mental images, for example, are really identical in meaning with statements about processes in the brain . . . Place's theory is that events of consciousness *happen* to be brain processes, as lightning *happens* to be an electrical discharge. (Grave 1984, 113)

This suggests that this theory is looking for a level on which events are *outside* meaning, a world of physical instances and real things where something can happen independent of any representation of it.

Brennan, too, must mean *not* that *time is compressed for space* and *producing profit* are identical in meaning, for they clearly have different meanings for us and relate to different discourses, but that the compression of time as space *happens* to be the production of profit, in the same sense that U.T. Place meant that events of consciousness *happen* to be brain processes.

An effect of the reduction of different discourses to a plane of coincidence is that it deprives Brennan and Place of the agency of rhetoric, whereas for Lacan this functions as an active element in the real. This may be why Brennan dwells on *writing* in the preface, since after all, meaning is the sticking point in such a reduction to the real.

To produce this account in the face of deconstruction, at the very least Brennan needs to show us that there is no ontological difference between generic orders. Yet what we know about signification, from Derrida and Foucault in particular, would tend to unglue this laminate of word and thing and allow a glimpse of how the sign points in the direction in which it fails.

The effort of combining the Marxist imagining with the Lacanian leads to the genuinely rhetorical struggle of the preface. Brennan writes:

> [*Interpretation of the Flesh* and *History After Lacan* were] drafted in a propositional mode; I shifted to the secondary mode in executing them, for reasons which are not all bad, except that too marked a preference for the secondary mode, and a reliance on established names in writing, are products of the social trend which my books were meant to analyse . . . The idea is simply that writing in a more propositional style goes against that era, to the extent that it shifts the fixed points on which the ego depends. (Brennan 1993, xi, xiii)

The suggestion that the rhetorical approach is itself embedded in the historical possibilities of the psyche, is both Lacanian and also goes beyond Lacan, invoking a geo-politics of reading, as well as a rhetoric of thought: "On the face of it, it seems easier to write in the propositional mode if one writes in France, while those who do not instead write secondary works elucidating, praising, or damning the propositions" (ibid., xiii). Brennan concludes these coincidental observations with the thought that the rhetorical might be dialectical: "The question of course is how to combine the propositional and secondary modes and thus transcend them" (ibid.).

The aporetic nature of the impasse of the subject as sign is not recoverable in sublation, Derrida and Deleuze seem to agree at least on this.[4] To put it another way, if energy were a thing, if "energy" was the currency of a reduction to a level of material before, behind or beyond our concepts of it, then there would certainly be no history.

I am tempted to say that Brennan is wrong, then, to abandon Lacan "at the foundation"; for without the Big "O" Other from which he drew so much bitter satisfaction, there is no signifying material. Specifically when he speaks of *jouissance*, Lacan points to an excess which is both material, i.e., energetic, and signifying (in that it is "beyond the phallus") and thus signifies the failure to signify. There is an excess which is an element in the *unpredictable*, the *resistance* of that which we have failed to capture in our concepts (even those concepts of physical, of material, and real); there is a kind of friction that comes of rubbing words over things.

> Thesis 6: *As the foundational fantasy is enacted on the large scale, as more and more objects are constructed in reality, the balance of energetic power, in relation to the generative chain of nature, has to shift. It shifts in terms of paradox. While the world appears to get faster and faster, it in fact gets slower and slower.* (Brennan 1993, 20)

This view of the present time judges it to be seriously "out of joint," changing toward a *telos* that has the feel of the apocalyptic about it.

Perhaps in the end we differ about time; then there is a time difference between Brennan and myself. By this I mean I cannot, myself, be in time in this way, in the "wrong" time zone. Put another way, speeding up or slowing down of time does not capture for me the real effects of signification. I need time on my side.

Notes

1. See Deleuze and Guattari (2000).

2. Question from the floor, on the occasion of John Searle's address to the Australasian Association of Philosophy 1988 annual conference, University of Queensland, Brisbane.

3. See also, Ferrell (1996), p. 69.

4. Cf. Gilles Deleuze, *Nietzsche and Philosophy*, trans. Hugh Tomlinson (New York: Columbia University Press, 1983) and Jacques Derrida, *Aporias*, trans. Thomas Dutoit (Stanford: Stanford University Press, 1993).

References

Brennan, Teresa. 1993. *History After Lacan*. New York and London: Routledge.

Deleuze, Gilles. 1996. *Difference and Repetition*. Paul Patton, trans. New York: Columbia University Press.

Deleuze, Gilles and Felix Guattari. 2000. *What is Philosophy?* Hugh Tomlinson & Graham Burchill, trans. London & New York: Verso

Derrida, Jacques. 1978. "The Ends of Man" in *Margins of Philosophy*. Alan Bass, trans. Chicago: University of Chicago Press. 109–114.

Easthope, Antony. 1995. "History and Psychoanalysis." *Textual Practice* 9(2): 349–398.

Ferrell, Robyn. 1996. *Passion in Theory*. New York and London: Routledge.

Grave, S.A. 1984. *A History of Philosophy in Australia*. St Lucia: University of Queensland Press.

Lacan, Jacques. 1977. *Ecrits: A Selection*. Alan Sheridan, trans. New York: Tavistock.

Place, U.T. 1956. "Is Consciousness a Brain Process?" *British Journal of Psychology* 47 (February).

Presley, C.F. 1971. *The Identity Theory of Mind, 2nd ed.* St Lucia: University of Queensland Press.

CHAPTER FOUR

Heidegger after Brennan

————— ❧ —————

Anne O'Byrne

THERE ARE MANY WAYS in which Teresa Brennan deliberately and explicitly set her work in relation to Heidegger's. In *Exhausting Modernity* (2000), her point of departure is "at least informed by . . . the critique of foundationalism begun by Heidegger" (Brennan 2000, 14). Throughout that work, as she builds her argument in readings of Marx, Freud and Lacan, Heidegger's name surfaces again and again showing his work to be a point of departure from which she does not quite depart, but which, rather continues to inform her readings of these others. For instance, she links his concern with the objectification of knowledge to Lacan's theory of the objectification of knowledge, his thought of the "standing reserve" to Marx's "standing army" and his critique of technology, more broadly speaking, to Benjamin's thinking of physics and metaphysics.

Indeed, in *History after Lacan* (1993), she puts it like this: "Heidegger, in this book, is a little like the butler. He comes on and off at the beginning and end of every chapter, he is obviously crucial although he does not star, and he probably did it" (Brennan 1993, 17). There are many who would be happy to agree that Heidegger did it; the problem is in figuring out just what *it* is. For Teresa Brennan, it involved undermining all assumptions that the subject is the starting point of ontology, which is also the assumption that the place occupied by the subject in the space of the world is what gives it this privileged position. This is the metaphysical thinking that Heidegger sought to overturn. But Brennan will insist it also involved far too much in the way of ontology, meaning that it happened on a level of abstraction that was not good. This is not to say that it is bad, but rather that Heidegger's investigation of the question of the meaning of Being is so abstract that the conclusions which follow from it "might lead anywhere." When Brennan makes this particular claim she does so in a vaguely threatening way which, along with a footnote citing Lacoue-Labarthe, suggests that that anywhere might very well be a distinctly bad somewhere.

33

She puts the same point more explicitly in *Exhausting Modernity*:

> [Heidegger] reads [the Anaximander fragment] in terms of how Being, as presence, requires withdrawal. In this, he is looking for a sphere beyond either a mechanistic understanding of nature on the one hand, or metaphysics on the other. But he looks for this sphere in the abstract, as do all who follow the flight from the flesh into metaphor. (Brennan 2000, 17n3)

Brennan discerns in Heidegger a thinker who shares her concern with nature and technology; she adds to that concern a Lacanian reading of the ego and a Lacan-inflected Marxist reading of the rise of capitalism, and then returns to the question of nature and technology in a way far more concrete than Heidegger ever could. Following another trajectory, she appreciates the ungrounding of the subject, and acknowledges that it specifically demands an interrogation of what grounds our psychic life, that is, the foundational fantasy.

The choice of terms is deliberate and idiosyncratic, and it is what must structure the re-reading of Heidegger. I will argue that the discussion of the foundational fantasy in fact leads us away from the thought of foundation to the thought of origin, and it also makes us confront Dasein's spatiality [*raumlichkeit*] specifically as embodiment. Together, questions of origin and of bodies direct us to a new reading of "generation," where the term is understood not just as a discrete stratum in the historical life of a people—as Heidegger would have it in *Being and Time*—but also as the very fleshy *process* of generation that is never far from Brennan's thoughts. It must be both/and. If we neglect the thought of generation from *Being and Time* (or something like it) we lose historical consciousness; if we neglect the process of generation, we find that we certainly are conscious of history, but only in abstract terms. In fact, it must be both/and because it cannot be either/or. After all, generations are generated. The problem for Heidegger, it would seem, is that he could think only half that thought.

This is not unlike the familiar criticism of Heidegger that he neglected the ontic in favor of the ontological, a critique so familiar that it seems hardly worth making any more. The difference here is that reading Heidegger after Brennan gives the point a finer focus and is thus far more useful than any broad rejection of ontology. It is a focus produced by the intersection of her concern 1) with the foundational fantasy as the foundation of the ego; 2) with the relation of that fantasy to technological development not to mention the rise of capitalism and imperialist expansion; and 3) with the role of the mother in the fantasy. Brennan's work, indebted as it is to Heidegger's rejection of metaphysical thinking, again makes the common point that the turn away from that mode of thought must eventually take into account the circumstances of our fleshly being-with-others-in-the-world. What is distinctly uncommon is the material her work provides for thinking this through.

I'll begin with a brief account of Heidegger's thought of generation and Brennan's argument (from *History after Lacan*) regarding the foundational fantasy. The problem Brennan delineates is addressed in certain re-readings of Heidegger's work, readings that lead us back to the thought of generation but in a way that delivers us not to a foundation but to an origin, which is to say, to a way of thinking that keeps Brennan's concerns alive and her thought in motion.

Heidegger on Generation

By Section 74 of *Being and Time*, Heidegger has already devoted a great deal of energy to doing those things for which Brennan praises him. He has been working to displace the subject as the central figure in our way of thinking, replacing it with Da-sein, being-there. He has begun to take apart the metaphysical thinking that later, in "The Question Concerning Technology," will bear the blame for our tendency to conceive ourselves over against nature, which in turn allows us to insist on our rightful domination of nature. He has also done a great deal of work on Dasein's temporality, but I would not agree that this is simply at the expense of its spatiality. After all, Dasein is *Da*, there; that particular spatial designation is utterly central to it. In addition, Heidegger's aim here is to set aside the standing metaphysical dichotomy of space and time and to show Dasein's being to be temporal being-in-the-world.

The fact that Dasein's being is being-in-the-world and the acknowledgement that this entails being-with-others together make clear Dasein's historicity as it is set out in Section 74. Heidegger has already analyzed Dasein's temporality in terms of anticipation and resoluteness in the face of what is to come in terms of the future. He has also made the claim that, contrary to common understanding, historicity must in turn be thought of not just in terms of the past and "having been" but also in terms of the present and the future. How does historizing operate? He writes:

> If fateful Dasein, as Being-in-the-world, exists existentially in Being-with-Others, its historizing is a co-historizing and is determinative for it as *destiny* . . . Destiny is not something that puts itself together out of individual fates, any more than Being-with-one-another can be conceived as the occurring together of several Subjects . . . Dasein's full destiny in and with its 'generation' goes to make up the full authentic historizing of Dasein. (H 384)[1]

Let me retrace this trajectory. Dasein's temporality is futural because of human finitude; our mode of being is Being-towards-death. Once we grasp this we become capable of authentic, resolute being. Throughout *Being and*

Time, this grasping has been presented as a being towards one's ownmost possibility. The death towards which I am is my own death, and no one can take over that death for me. What is added with the thought of historicity is the acknowledgement that my Being-in-the-world is a being-with-others; that being-with-others is experienced as authentic historicity when it is experienced as part of a generation.

But human finitude has as much to do with the fact of our having been born, and thus also our capacity to beget and give birth, as it has to do with death. We are natal and reproductive, as well as mortal beings, and this is also granted, obliquely and reluctantly, by Heidegger's mention of generation here. What is significant is not only that I die, but that I am followed by others, not only that we will all die but that this generation will be succeeded by another.

Theodore Kisiel, one of the few Heidegger scholars to study this issue, insists that at no point is this a thought of biological generation. Rather, he argues, what Heidegger has in mind (as he indicates in a footnote in *Being and Time*) is Dilthey's definition of a generation as a group of near contemporaries who by undergoing together the great questions and changes of their day, form a bond and a group that maintains heterogeneity while uniting its members. *"Eine Schule"* is the term he uses (Kisiel 2001, 90), and the example he supplies is the generation of Novalis, Schleiermacher, Hölderlin and Hegel, the second generation of the German Enlightenment. The great event that would have bound them might have been the French Revolution, and the phenomena of Napoleon and his campaigns, just as the event that formed the generation of Heidegger, Scheler, and Juenger was the experience of the First World War. Kisiel first sees Heidegger in those post-war years reflecting on the meaning of generation and the process by which a generation follows on another. The initial concern, he argues, seems to have been anything but abstract. Rather, Heidegger saw the way things stood with a student body that included a great number of men who had been in the trenches. He saw their *weltmuedigkeit*; and he saw in the youth and student movements of the time, for instance, the Deutsche Akademische Freischar group, a generation coming to recognize itself as such and to grasp what it meant for a generation to come into its own.[2]

Heidegger is not wholly or not always, given over to sheer abstraction. Yet, along with this concrete concern comes a troublesome distinction that allows Kisiel to conclude that "the real 'ontological place' of a generation is thus socio-historical life and not, as sociologist August Comte would have it, biological life" (Kisiel 2001, 91). This is the sort of claim that Teresa Brennan would relish taking apart. It is no longer as simple as a flight from the flesh into abstraction, but rather a failure to understand that the flesh is a social, political, historical, biological, psychological phenomenon.

Foundations and Fantasy

In *Exhausting Modernity*, Brennan acknowledges that her treatment of the foundational fantasy has its place in the post-Heideggerian conversation. Heidegger's critique of foundationalism set her thinking under way, and she makes clear her understanding of that critique:

> Everything criticized under the rubric of 'foundationalism' depends on the assumption that the human being is the privileged origin of meaning, intelligence and truth. This is why I have borrowed the term 'foundational' to describe the fantasy. But I stress that using the term foundational does not mean that there are no 'foundations.' (Brennan 2000, 14)

That is to say, "foundational fantasy" is a term that Brennan understands as allowing her to reject the claim that the autonomous human subject is the source of meaning but to posit (not to say postulate) a natural, generative foundation that sustains life and is itself capable of granting meaning. It is clear how Heidegger's thought could set such thinking in motion despite readings that drive a wedge between the ontic and the ontological. But it is not clear that it could sustain it given the abyss, the ungrounded ground, that Heidegger encounters once he opens the question of the meaning of Being.

It is in *History After Lacan* that Brennan sets out her thesis, clearly and most forcefully. There is, she argues, a fantasy by which the subject founds itself, and it requires turning its environment into an object. That is to say, following Melanie Klein, that the mother's body is transformed into an object. The subject goes on to imagine itself as "energetically contained," a discrete being essentially distinct from its environment for whom, therefore, the experience of an energetic connection to its environment is foreclosed. It also goes on to fantasize the domination/control/dismemberment of the objectified environment/maternal body.

In the course of time, technology has created the opportunity for the foundational fantasy to take hold on a global scale, and this is where Heidegger makes one of his butler-style appearances. He describes the problem at the heart of the phenomenon of technological domination of nature as the metaphysical mindset, a mode of thinking that always regards the subject and its relation to its present space as primary. That makes possible the gross exploitation of nature, threatening to convert it all, famously, into a standing reserve. Brennan quotes Heidegger approvingly, adding only that it is a mindset better described as foundational. By privileging space over time, the metaphysical/foundational mindset allows the subject to conceive itself as its own creator, as giving birth to itself, and to thereby repress consciousness of history and the historical process.

Brennan goes on to argue that the foundational fantasy itself requires a foundation before the foundation, one that is conceived in non-subjective terms: "The foundational fantasy is not fantasmic because there is no foundation. It is fantasmic because of the illusory foundations it structures and proceeds to make material, which overlie the natural generative foundation with which it competes" (Brennan 1993, 16). Heidegger now appears again as Brennan wonders whether or not he rules out all foundations, even non-subjective ones. Probably not, she says, but cuts short the speculation with the comment, by now familiar, that his work is too abstract in any case. This is the force of the *probably* in her comment that "he probably did it." She asks the most interesting questions, but, like a perspicacious but distracted detective, she doesn't bring the butler in for questioning. The mystery she most cares about has more to do with the sweat and life in the workers' cottages than with the thin air of the drawing room.

It is in the workers' cottages that the technological triumph of the foundational fantasy is deeply, if not always consciously, experienced. Technology under capitalism has found a way to satisfy the desires of the foundational fantasy, but it does so by taking natural substance and energy—raw material and labor in a more conventional, Marxist register—and binding them in commodities at a rate faster than nature can reproduce. The tendency in such a system will always be to constantly expand the territory under its control, hence imperialism and globalization, to speed up the rate of reproduction and to exhaust nature, including ourselves as workers. In the terminology of Heidegger's "Question Concerning Technology," we become a standing reserve, reduced to the mode of being of equipment lying ready to hand. Thus by reading the operation of the fantasy, first described as a foundation for the developing psyche in the mother-child relationship, in the functioning of macro-economic forces, Brennan works to undo any analyses that force a strict distinction between the socio-historical and the biological.

Brennan has described the illusory foundations, structured by the foundational fantasy, as overlying the natural generative foundation, with which the fantasy competes (Brennan 1993, 16). She acknowledges that this description rests on an assumption that living natural reality exists and, more importantly, she agrees that knowledge of it is confused by the fantasmic overlay. Indeed, living reality itself becomes confused. She goes on:

> I also assume that one result of the social coverage is to make one doubt the existence of an unchanging reality, precisely because connections with that reality are severed and reality is changed. But even if the world becomes an 'as if' fantasmic world, it does not follow that this is the only possible world . . . [I]t does not mean that the constructed world of fantasies cannot be differentiated in principle from a living reality. (Ibid., 21)

So while insistent that we reject mere abstraction and return to the material level, Brennan is under no illusion that social constructions can be set aside, giving open access to natural reality, nor is she willing to say that they are so inextricably linked as to be effectively the same. She would not describe the life she wants to examine as socio-politico-historico-psycho-biological. I think she would prefer to think of it as social and political and historical and psychological and biological.

Because Brennan's main concerns are making the connection between micro and macro levels and identifying the conditions that make possible alienation and exploitation, it is obvious why she should choose to establish her link to Heidegger through his essay devoted explicitly to technology. Yet if she were to seriously pursue the question of Heidegger's rejection of foundations, a reading of "The Origin of the Work of Art" might prove more fruitful. She sees Heidegger as doing the right thing when he displaces not just the subject but the subject/object distinction, and he is lauded for undermining the metaphysical/foundational mindset by reviving the thought of our temporality. The problem, she concludes, is that in doing so he never reaches to the level of what she calls the generative chain of nature, and so his work misses the mark. Or does it?

Dasein's Spatiality, Dasein's Origin

Having read Brennan, what happens if we return to Heidegger now? There is difficulty in the fact that she has praised and blamed him for what appears to be the same thing, or at least sides of the same coin—his shift from a metaphysical concern with spatiality to a concern with temporality on the one hand and his flight from the flesh and the level of the concrete and material world on the other. After all, Dasein's concreteness must be its spatiality. Early in *Being and Time*, Heidegger does seem to ward off any such interpretation, saying: "Dasein's spatiality is not to be thought in terms of its bodily nature, founded in turn on corporeality" (H 89). This, on first reading, seems to mean that Dasein is *dis*embodied and indeed that Dasein may not be thought of as embodied; but I do not think this is the case. What Heidegger rejects here is the dichotomy that sets corporeality in opposition to spirituality. Later, in S. 70, he writes: "[Dasein] is by no means just present-at-hand in a bit of space which its body fills up" (H 368). Does *this* not mean that we may not think of an embodied Dasein? Again, I think not. What Heidegger rejects here is the thought of Dasein's body as something that takes up space in the world the way a piece of equipment or a lump of earth might. Rather, he says, rejecting the old Cartesian model, our bodies are "spatial in a way which remains essentially impossible for any extended corporeal thing" (ibid.).

These are still only indications of what Dasein's spatiality is not. When it comes to a positive designation, the best we can find is this: "Dasein can be spatial only as care, in the sense of existing as factically falling" (H 368). It would take a work far longer than this present essay to give all the content of this sentence its due; so it must suffice to read it three times here. First, reading with Jean-Luc Nancy, the sentence's reference to falling suggests turning to the concept of origin that appears in "The Origin of the Work of Art" and in the use of *originarity* in *Being and Time*. In a move which could be described as a shift from *fundamental* ontology to *originary* ontology, Nancy investigates the origin of Dasein. Second, following Peg Birmingham's Arendtian reading, we see that Dasein's *raumlichkeit* or spatiality is indeed its embodiment, but not simply or merely so. Third, reading with David Wood, it becomes clear that Dasein's fallen-ness is a *falling*; that is to say, Dasein is the sort of being that is subject to change and transformation.

At the opening of "The Origin of the Work of Art," Heidegger writes: "Origin here means that from which and by which something is what it is and as it is" (Heidegger 1993a, 143). Brennan, Nancy and Heidegger all make use of the terminology of origin and of foundation or fundament. We have seen Brennan describe *foundationalism* as the insistence that the human being is the *origin* of meaning; Nancy writes that *originary* alterity is at the *foundation* of Being (Nancy 2000, 12); Heidegger points out that his *fundamental* ontology must also be *originary* (H 232).[3] The relationship between the two registers and the two ways of thinking is complex and varies greatly in the works of these three writers. But, crudely put, foundation has the character of a monolithic substratum that has been completed and upon which a superstructure rests, while *origin* retains connotations of an active, generative source that is, at least in Nancy's analysis, necessarily plural.

In *Being Singular Plural*, Nancy's concern is with (paraphrasing Heidegger) that from which and by which *we* are what we are and as we are. This is an ontology, and the language is the sort of abstract Heidegger-ese that Brennan despised; but it is also the case that Nancy's "ontological attestations" all emerge from reflection on common events. For instance, he describes the way we look into a new baby's face to see who she looks like, or how we recognize someone in a snapshot; what we experience in such moments is "the passage of other origins of the world" (Nancy 2000, 9). It is not that there are many origins, or that the origin is shattered or divided, but rather that it is shared and shared out among all beings. He writes:

> We have access to the truth of the origin as many times as we are in one another's presence and in the presence of the rest of beings . . . It is never a question of full access, access to the whole of the origin. *Origin* does not

signify that from which the world comes, but rather the coming of each presence of the world, each time singular. (Ibid., 13–15)

Such thought of origin avoids foundationalism as Brennan defines it by virtue of identifying the source of meaning in beings and in each being, not in the human being. That is to say, the source of meaning must be singular and plural too; Dasein (being-there) is co-originary with Mitsein (being-with). Yet the formulation of this thought that resonates most clearly with Brennan's work, reminding us of her intersubjective economy of energy,[4] though exploding the mere intersubjectivity of it, uses the language of circulation:

> There is no other meaning than the meaning of circulation. But this circulation goes in all directions at once, in all the directions of all the space-times opened by presence to presence: all things, all beings, all entities, everything past and future, alive dead, inanimate, stones, plants, nails, gods—and "humans," that is, those who expose sharing and circulation as such by saying "we," by *saying we to themselves* in all possible senses of that expression, and by saying we for the totality of all being. (Ibid., 3)

There is no place here for the monolithic foundation, but there is scope for developing what is a deeply Heideggerian thought in the direction of the thought, so characteristic of Brennan's ontology, of beings who come to be and exist with and between.

The sentence, "Dasein can be spatial only as care, in the sense of existing as factically falling" (H 368), reminds us that we emerge into a world made up of and by others. Arendt puts it most pointedly when she insists, in *The Human Condition*, on the significance of birth. When we read the sentence for the second time we are reminded that we come into the world from another being in the most material, fleshy way imaginable, and our being here is necessarily being-with. Arendt goes on to work very hard to set aside the fleshy-ness of this fact and to deal instead in terms of a second nature that is indicated by this first nature, which is her attempt to set the political and the historical apart from the biological and the social. It goes on to produce deep problems for her political project. However, in her essay "Heidegger and Arendt: The Birth of Political Action and Speech," Birmingham takes up Arendt's concerns pointing out that there are resources in *Being and Time* that Arendt neglected, resources that would help overcome the split. After all, Dasein's being-spatial is experienced as embodiment; she goes on to indicate the sense in which Dasein is always at a distance from itself as embodied. This is the force of Dasein's fallen-ness, and it is the indication that this is something other than mere biology. Dasein is always in relation to itself. It is never self-identical and is never at one with its own material being in the way that any mere present-at-hand being is. Heidegger's term is *Entfernung*, Dasein's

De-severence, its proximity to and distance from itself that never reaches the state of accomplished self-identity.

David Wood, in his essay "Reading Heidegger Responsibly: Glimpses of Being in Dasein's Development," pursues his characteristic concern with temporality towards the thought that we are beings who pass through stages of development. After all, falling must also involve movement and change. Our being embodied is our being subject to change and transformation and this is the spatial-temporal fact of our finitude. We are not finite in any simple way in the sense that we do not come to be and pass away without undergoing deep transformations in between. Wood argues that, on the basis of Dasein's temporality, one can make the case for the transcendental significance of childhood and human development. In fact, he believes that thinking about development can allow us to "illuminate many of the claims Heidegger wants to make, and . . . [that] this developmental perspective gives Heidegger's thinking a new future" (Wood 2002, 225).

The specific Heideggerian claims Wood works to shed light on include the thought that philosophy is born from the pain of transition and renewal, that individual development has some of the same kinds of traumatic transformations that we find in human history, and that our own memories show us the difficulty of access to the past.

Here we begin to find ourselves in Brennan territory. According to Wood, all of this moves to a point already a commonplace in psychoanalysis: "That structural transformations are inherent in human development, that humans are essentially developmental creatures, and that these developments are incomplete" (Wood 2002, 229). If we add the thought of generation here, and the fact that we arrive into the world from our mothers, we begin to understand that Dasein's fallen-ness is an experience permeated by loss. This is what gives us the intimation (and here I paraphrase Wood responding to Derrida remarking on Lacan) that transitions are potentially abyssal; this is why we experience them as angst; this is how they give us a lived experience of extinction and indeed death. Wood concludes that "human development is a fundamentally incomplete ontological journey" (ibid., 232). This is the thought that should serve to unfound any foundational fantasy, and it has its origin precisely in Dasein's embodied, temporal being.

The point where these readings can be drawn together—Dasein as inevitably, originarily with others, as non-identical with itself, as worldly, as subject to transformation—is, finally, the thought of generation. Brennan is right; the thought never quite manages to grant access to a foundation on the level of generative nature. This is because Heidegger would indeed reject all thought of foundation, preferring, in its stead, the thought of origin, a lively, generative, singular, plural origin that may turn out to be capable of addressing many of Brennan's concerns without fading away into mere abstraction.

Conclusion

My speculation here has been that if Brennan questioned the butler, she might find out that he did more, though perhaps in an obscure sort of way, than either the detective or the butler himself realized. One of Brennan's most valuable achievements is in drawing the connection between the subject's way of being—that is, the foundational fantasy—and modern patterns of domination. Heidegger can certainly be described as having done that, but not in the same way. He set aside the mode of thinking built in terms of foundation and superstructure, a scheme deeply unsuited to the analysis of the beings we are and itself implicated in those patterns of domination. He displaced the subject and subject-centred spatiality, and then reintroduced spatiality as Dasein's de-severed embodiment. The fact that Dasein is Being-in-the-world and is natal means that it is never removed from others or from the world in the way that the subject—the product of the foundational fantasy—conceives itself to be. At the same time, the fact that Dasein is an embodied being-there, that it is temporal as well as spatial, means that its being is inevitably subject to changes that are all potentially abyssal and ungrounding. Finally, all of this comes together in the sort of social, biological, historical, political, psychological re-reading of Heidegger's thought of generation that I have gestured towards here—a reading that will be complex, and difficult to make clear, but one that becomes our task after Brennan.

Notes

1. References to *Being and Time* are to the translation listed below, and take the form (H 123), using the page numbers of the German Meiner edition listed in the margins of the translation.

2. This foreshadows the *Rektoratsrede* of 1933 and Heidegger's most intimate connection with Nazism.

3. *Originary* here translates *ursprunglich*, which is translated by Maquarrie and Robinson as *primordial*.

4. See Brennan's *Exhausting Modernity*, pp. 64–65.

References

Birmingham, Peg. 2002. "Heidegger and Arendt: The Birth of Political Action and Speech" in *Heidegger and Practical Philosophy*. Francois Raffoul and David Pettigrew, eds. New York: Humanities Press, 191–218.

Brennan, Teresa. 2000. *Exhausting Modernity: Grounds for a New Economy*. London: Routledge.

———1993. *History after Lacan*. London: Routledge.

Heidegger, Martin. 1996. *Being and Time*. Joan Stambaugh, trans. New York: State University of New York Press.

———1993a. "The Origin of the Work of Art," trans. Albert Hofstadter in *Basic Writings*. David Farrell Krell, ed. New York: Harper Collins, 143–212.

———1993b. "The Question Concerning Technology," trans. William Lovitt in *Basic Writings*. David Farrell Krell, ed. New York: Harper Collins, 308–341.

Kisiel, Theodore. 2001. "Der sozio-logische Komplex der Geschichtlichkeit des Daseins: Volk, Gemeinschaft, Generation," in *Die Jemeinigkeit des Mitseins: Die Daseinsanalytik Martin Heideggers und die Kritik der soziologischen Vernunft*. Johannes Weiss, ed. Konstanz: UVK Verlagsgesellschaft mBH, 85–103.

Nancy, Jean-Luc. 2000. *Being Singular Plural*. Robert Richardson and Anne O'Byrne, trans. Stanford: Stanford University Press.

Wood, David. 2002. "Reading Heidegger Responsibly: Glimpses of Being in Dasein's Development," in *Heidegger and Practical Philosophy*. Francois Raffoul and David Pettigrew, eds. New York: Humanities Press, 219–235.

CHAPTER FIVE

Repressed Knowledge and the Transmission of Affect

———— ❦ ————

Susan James

I LAST SAW TERESA BRENNAN when she passed through England in the summer of 2002 on her way to Israel, where she was planning to join a group of academics visiting the West Bank. As things turned out, she set off on the next stage of her journey via Egypt, and was surprised and somewhat crestfallen when even her formidable powers of persuasion failed to move the Egyptian authorities to allow her to fly from Alexandria to Tel Aviv. So she never got to Israel after all. But before that adventure, she and her daughter Sangi made a trip from London to stay with us in Cambridge. Teresa arrived in good spirits, ready to drink champagne and talk at length. Among the many subjects we discussed during that twenty-four hours, so poignantly precious in retrospect, was the book she was just finishing, *The Transmission of Affect* (2004). Conceived as part of an encompassing critique of contemporary western societies, and designed to reveal the interconnections between their biological, economic, psychological and political failings, this volume belonged to a trilogy aimed, in a way, to out-Marx Marx. It was completed shortly before Teresa died and weaves together several of the most resonant themes of her life and work. Reflecting on it is a way of remembering her, celebrating her, and mourning her loss.

The transmission of affect is a problem that troubled Teresa in her everyday life. She was, I think, exceptionally sensitive to ambient affects, sometimes suddenly exhilarated by the feel of a conversation, sometimes deeply dismayed by the atmosphere of a room. There were times when these feelings so overwhelmed her that she became deaf to other cues, to the conversations around her, to ordinary courtesies like, "Would you like some more salad?," and so on. She also used to worry about such feelings. Were they straightforwardly hers? If they came from other people, was she interpreting them accurately? When they felt hostile, was she exaggerating them? If not, what was it about her that attracted them? So it's not surprising that she wanted to understand the transmission of affect and trace its implications for some of our conceptions of the self.

Her investigation of these problems is organized around two opposing strands of thought. According to the first, which she takes to be a contemporary commonplace, our affects are our own. They are generated within the individual subject and are the fruits of its experience and history, so that to understand them is to understand how individuals create them. The second strand contends, by contrast, that at least some of our affects come from outside. They are things that happen to us rather than things we do, and we are passive in the face of them. However, for this account to be right, passions or affects that originate elsewhere have somehow got to get inside us.

The history of this latter view is as long as the western philosophical tradition, and is embedded both in the vocabulary we use to talk about the emotions—in the English term "passion" and its many cognates—and in the metaphors through which we characterize them, as when we are swept away by anger, overcome by fear, or eaten up by envy. It is surely right to say that a passive conception of the emotions has largely gone out of fashion, and that whether they are conscious or unconscious, destructive or enabling, they are widely assumed to be among our own responses to ourselves and the world. In urging us to resist this established consensus and reconsider the ancient claim that our passions are in some sense external in origin, Teresa touches a revisionist nerve within current intellectual debate. She offers an uncompromising defence of the view that our affects can be caused by passions that others transmit to us, presenting this claim as a viable scientific hypothesis, and also as a valuable moral insight. Our concern with our own boundedness and our understanding of ourselves as separate, autonomous individuals prevents us from discriminating between transmitted and non-transmitted affects. This repression blocks our ability to gain an adequate understanding of our emotions, which in turn diminishes the quality of our individual and collective lives.

In developing this line of argument, *The Transmission of Affect* modulates through many different keys. Like a sonata by Brahms, it is continually on the move, and the restlessness of the journey so undermines the completeness of the final resolution that home, when we finally arrive at it, does not feel quite like home any longer. Reading through the book, one encounters a deliberately dislocated form, which moves without explanation from one mode of argument to another—from popular science to group psychology, to psychoanalysis, and ultimately to a moral and theological vision of a wiser and more harmonious way of life. To understand these transitions, it is helpful to think of them as marking the moments where the author turns from one audience to another, to think of the book as an ambitious and synthesizing effort to shape a sequence of social imaginaries by inserting the transmission of affect into various distinct narratives and schemes of value. It sets out to win the attention and sympathy of scientists, historians, philosophers, psychoanalysts, phenomenologists, and theologians, addressing each in their own language and offering them a seductive sketch of further lines of enquiry.

To disarm the scepticism of an empirically minded community, Teresa first confronts the nagging question, "But how does transmission of affect actually work?" Not, she claims, by visual sensation, which we understand as stopping at the surface of the body and leaving it unaltered and intact; but rather by smell, or more precisely by hormonal exchanges. There really is a stink of fear that can excite aggression and an odor of sanctity that can generate devotion or contempt; we need to use scientific forms of investigation to fill out the truths captured in such images. The hypothesis that emotions can be smelled, preliminary as it is, aims to draw scientists into the project by formulating it in terms that fit and challenge their programs of research. Supportive and critical by turns, Teresa takes a position within a broadly biological set of debates and proposes a line of empirical investigation that might advance them.

Turning to a more familiar arena and to a group of readers working in the psychoanalytic tradition, *The Transmission of Affect* next builds on the argument of Teresa's earlier book, *History After Lacan* (1993), by figuring affective relationships as transfers of energy that enhance or impede the force of the life drive. The transfer of affect from one person to another plays a crucial role in explaining the projections that constitute the foundational fantasy, in which the infant projects its own powerlessness on to the mother and attributes the mother's power and agency to itself. It does this, by taking a flow of energy that originates in the mother as its own, and claiming for itself an affect which is in fact transmitted to it from outside. Here, by tacitly identifying the energy that flows between mother and child with an exchange of hormones, and grounding the development of an infant's psychic capacities on a physical process, Teresa portrays natural scientists and psychoanalysts as co-workers, investigating a single phenomenon in two vocabularies.

The role of the transmission of affect in projection means that its significance extends beyond the foundational fantasy itself to the reenactments of it that are the stuff of everyday psychic life, and through which we maintain ourselves as bounded subjects. In addition, it extends to particular patterns of projection, such as the transference and countertransference between analyst and patient. Drawing us on a little, and now widening her audience to include sociologists and physicians, Teresa suggests that transmission can explain a number of further puzzles. It may, for example, offer a more fruitful account of crowd behavior than the explanations currently available. It may help to explain certain psychosomatic diseases and cast light on barely acknowledged evidence about the psychic relationship between fetuses and their birth mothers.

Some of the readers that this argument aims to persuade will wonder whether there is any historical evidence of the transmission of affect. This can be found, the book proposes, in medieval portrayals of passions as the work of demons that manipulate the body and create deviant affects, and in early-modern accounts of passions as motions of the animal spirits which interact with the movements of less rarefied kinds of matter. The recitation of this kind of evidence ushers in a more moralizing strand of argument, a lament, if you like, for a form of self-understanding that was once part of European culture, but has since been repressed. To maintain our conception of the bounded self in the face of the affects we transmit and those transmitted to us, we have repressed our consciousness of the fact of transmission, thus constructing the borderline between subject and object. Only this fantasy generates our illusion of completeness, which is reflected in, and sustained by, the intellectual work of philosophers, economists, psychologists, and others. Turning to these benighted souls, Teresa questions their conviction that the mind takes priority over the body in the explanation of emotion, and their adamant demotion of forms of knowledge that challenge this orthodoxy. Egoic as we have become, we conceive of the mind as a haven in which the affects can be safely protected from the bodily realm, and are content to work with the notion of an individual who calculates from a position of self-interest.

Teresa's criticisms of this stance are indebted to her own feminist formation as a student at the University of Sydney. Her interest in the transmission of affect pivots around the re-evaluation of mind and body that has been so important in the work of a group of Australian philosophers such as Ros Diprose, Moira Gatens, Elizabeth Grosz, Genevieve Lloyd, and Carole Pateman. Another of the imaginaries that *The Transmission of Affect* is trying not so much to alter as to enrich is that of feminist philosophy. It builds on the discourse of the past twenty-five years or so to press home its claim that a conception of the self as embodied and weakly-bounded cries out for an accompanying account of affective relationships, capable of doing justice to our imperfectly articulated knowledge of the way passions move around. To recapture an understanding of the mobility of our own affects, or even to recognize that there is anything to be understood, we need to cultivate what Teresa calls discernment—the power to feel with our bodies the difference between transmitted and non-transmitted affects. Until we can recover this skill, we are fated to live with an exhausting repression, through which the self is identified with its affects, and its affects are embraced as authentic, regardless of where they originated.

A work that speaks to such diverse audiences, links such a range of projects, and aims to raise as well as answer questions—*The Transmission of Affect* is perhaps best seen as a cornucopia in which readers will discover different pleasures, problems, and ideas with which to conjure. If so, it will have fulfilled its goal. I find myself excited by its claim that a conscious awareness of the transmission of affect was repressed during the eighteenth century, and keen to understand more clearly what conscious knowledge is supposed to have been lost.

As the book explains, there were in the late seventeenth century various theories about the circumstances in which passions could enter a person from outside. The experiences of pregnant women might affect the temperaments, as well as the bodies, of the fetuses in their wombs.[1] Children were more vulnerable to their emotional environments than adults because of the softness of their bodily fibres[2]; and adults with exceptional imaginations sometimes received into their bodies fluxes or vapours exhaled by other people or even by things. For example, a recent study of Jacques Aymar, a dowser who was apparently able to find murderers as well as water with his dowsing rod, traces the debate between those seventeenth-century observers who were convinced that the violent agitations suffered by Aymar when he identified a criminal were mechanically transmitted to him, and those who attributed his affects to the intervention of a demon.[3] (These two kinds of explanation were not historically sequential, as *The Transmission of Affect* suggests, but came to exist alongside one another.)

What preoccupied the advocates of these hypotheses was not whether passions could be transmitted, but rather how transmission occurred. Yet it is important that, in all these cases, the capacity to transmit or receive affects is treated as exceptional, and to some degree suspect. Pregnancy gave a woman a dangerous power to transfer her affects and damage the fetus she was carrying; and a fetus, like a child, needed protection because it had not yet acquired the strength to protect itself. By contrast, adult men and women were usually proof against irregular invasions of affect and generally possessed what was regarded as a normal level of resistance, against which deviations from the norm were measured. To experience migrating passions, an individual, whether a dowser or a prophet, had to be unusually sensitive. And when a whole community 'caught' a passionate infection in an outbreak of religious enthusiasm, a special explanation was required.

These analyses of transmission, which rely on a distinction between the normal and the pathological, are grounded on an assumption that Teresa rejects, namely that, "the capacity to resist . . . unwanted affects is . . . based on the boundaries that 'healthy' persons are said to possess and 'unhealthy' ones lack" (Brennan 2004, 11). The doctors, theologians, or philosophers who postulated fluxes or demons to explain the phenomena they encountered tended to regard their subjects with the condescension of the reliable for the wayward, and of the psychically resilient for the emotionally delicate. Although they accepted the existence of the transmission of affect, and thus agreed that passions can enter the body from outside, they did not seem to acknowledge the "normal" transmissions of negative affects with which Teresa is concerned.

To find any recognition of the projections that formed her central preoccupation, we do best to turn to early-modern discussions of the way that the passions of esteem and contempt travel between "inferior" and "superior" individuals or groups. Although this is not the only source of early modern evidence available, I believe it provides the clearest and sharpest illustration of the patterns of projection that Teresa identifies. As she notes, some seventeenth-century philosophers interpret the esteem and contempt that two unequal people may feel for one another in physical terms, as a mechanical exchange which alters the bodies of both parties and is manifested in their gestures, posture, and so on.[4] Moreover, authors who do not trouble to analyze the mechanisms by which affects are transmitted nevertheless agree that passionate exchanges occur and have bodily effects. The self-esteem of a superior, such as a prince, is fortified by the admiration of an inferior, such as a courtier, and is manifested in the prince's bearing, while the courtier's sense of his own worth is both reinforced by his association with the prince and put under pressure by the prince's contempt for him. The fascination of early modern writers with this type of exchange, and their appreciation of its function in sustaining a sense of self, indicates that they were keenly aware of the phenomena that Teresa describes as reenactments of the foundational fantasy. This aspect of their interpretation of transmission therefore provides support not only for the claim that the mobility of affects was understood in the seventeenth century, but that the role of physically transmitted affects in upholding a sense of self was also comprehended and theorized.

If we ask how these normal exchanges of passion were evaluated by early-modern writers, we encounter a variety of replies, only some of which resonate with the argument of *The Transmission of Affect*. Teresa's final chapter, in which she advocates the cultivation of discernment as a way to maintain an adequately bounded sense of self, while overcoming the debilitation involved in reiterating the foundational fantasy, can be read as a reworking of an attractive line of thought that is most prominent in the work of Spinoza. Like her, Spinoza views the negative affects as disempowering, and regards the passionate processes in which they are created or exchanged as liable to be debilitating.[5] As Spinoza illustrates, individuals exposed to the hatred of others will find themselves hating in return, and when the loves that sustain us are threatened we suffer envy.[6] Such passions diminish our power to maintain ourselves; or, as Teresa points out, the need to sustain the ego by projecting our negative affects takes up a great deal of energy. According to Spinoza, the only way out of this bind is to improve one's understanding of the causal processes in which our passions are enmeshed, by coming to recognize them as empowering or disempowering responses to a world with which we are continually interacting, and by which we are continually being changed. This sort of knowledge will not get rid of our affects, but it can change them, and in doing so strengthen our resistance to passions that are liable to be individually or collectively destructive.

Teresa's discussion of discernment fits easily into this model since it explores one of the forms that Spinoza's notion of understanding might take. She argues that, in order to resist the debilitation that transmitted passions generate, we need to acquire a greater sensitivity to the meanings of the bodily changes they bring about. Rather in the same way that Spinoza takes it that humans are naturally disposed to experience negative affects and must learn to deal with them, so she assumes that passionate interaction is fundamental to the establishment of the self. Individuals must live out the foundational fantasy before they can begin to correct the distortions to which it gives rise. But these distortions can be overcome, because there exists a more energizing way to maintain the boundary around the self.

Of all seventeenth-century writers, Spinoza provides the strongest support for Teresa's claim that there was in this era a conscious awareness not only of the transmission of affect, but also of the damage done by what she describes as the projection of negative affects. Although Spinoza's contemporaries shared his conviction that humans are in principle capable of modifying their affective dispositions for the better, some of them remained more attached than he did to the advantages of what they regarded as normal forms of passionate transmission. Malebranche, for example, concedes that our affects are a regrettable feature of our fallen condition, while simultaneously admiring their divinely ordained economy. All passions serve some beneficial purpose, so that, for example, our disposition to admire our superiors and feel contempt for our inferiors not only helps to maintain our individual sense of self, but also sustains the hierarchical forms of social and political organization for which the divinity has fitted us.[7] Our need for admiration and its role in bolstering our sense of self is best met in carefully co-ordinated societies organized around rank and privilege. So whether passionate exchange was regarded as valuable or dangerous was partly a political matter. Therefore debates about it contained a political dimension that is not directly addressed in *The Transmission of Affect*.

Seventeenth-century theorists were not only aware of the exchanges of passion through which individuals maintain themselves in the course of everyday life; many of them also distinguished acceptable from dangerous transmissions of affect and viewed the former as a valuable if imperfect means of maintaining individual stability and political order.

Teresa's emphasis on the energy wasted in projecting negative affects, and her desire to delineate a way of life freed as far as possible from the destructive legacy of the foundational fantasy, diminishes her concern with the positive features of affective transmission. Although she continues to remind us that individuals must project in order to maintain the boundaries that keep them from psychosis on one side and neurosis on the other, she is less interested in exploring social and political ways of satisfying this need than in seeing how to side-step it through the cultivation of discernment. This is a lacuna in her own position; in order to develop her stance one would need to deal more thoroughly with the difference between productive and destructive forms of projection. But it is also a focus of interest that may help to explain why she does not pause to examine the ambivalence with which the transmission of affect was regarded in the early-modern culture of the west. On the one hand, affective exchanges were held to threaten harmonious relations and diminish human powers; on the other hand, they sustained the social order. By neglecting the second view, Teresa is led to the dubious judgment that conscious knowledge of the transmission of affect was lost in the course of the eighteenth century, thus running together a series of distinct questions about what now needs to be recovered.

One of the staples of seventeenth-century moral psychology, which survived and flourished in the succeeding century, was the view that our passionate exchanges are organized around the twin dispositions to compare ourselves with others, and to sympathize with them.[8] As we have already seen, the disposition to compare underlies the passions of esteem and contempt, along with a family of related affects such as humility, admiration, and respect. By measuring ourselves against people who are invested with some mark of relative inferiority, we are able to project our own sense of inadequacy in the guise of contempt. The more needy we are, the more we depend on hierarchical practices that provide opportunities for different kinds of people to uphold a tolerable sense of self. At the same time, humans are held to be disposed to sympathize with the passions of others and to respond to their joy with delight, and their sorrow with pity or compassion. Transmission is therefore not confined to the negative affects, and, as Teresa acknowledges, a capacity to dump one's unwanted passions on someone else is matched by a capacity to sustain those around us by sympathizing with them. Humans are prone to identify as well as compete with each other, and to recognize continuity as well as difference.

These complementary yet opposed forms of transmission are carefully explored by a series of influential eighteenth-century writers who take it for granted that emotions evoke answering emotions. To cite the briefest of examples, Hume comments that our ability "to receive by communication the inclinations and sentiments [of others], however different from, or opposed to, our own," makes our minds "mirrors to one another" (Hume 1978, 631). Likewise, Adam Smith, in the discussion of sympathy with which he opens his *Theory of Moral Sentiments*, urges that, "whatever is the passion which arises from any object in the person principally concerned, an analogous emotion springs up, at the thought of his situation, in the breast of every attentive spectator." So much so, that "the passions, on some occasions, seem to be . . . transfused from one man to another, instantaneously, and antecedent to what excited them in the person principally concerned" (Smith 1976, 10–11). Therefore it cannot be conscious knowledge of the transmission of passion as such that is lost in the eighteenth century. Nor can it be straightforwardly true that the recognition that some passions originate outside us is successfully repressed. Nevertheless, there are changes in this period that are pertinent to Teresa's interpretation, and examining them will help to clarify her thesis about the history of the repressions that sustain the ego.

Rather than trying to identify physical mechanisms underlying the transmission of passion, many eighteenth-century philosophers are content to argue that the communication of an affect from one person to another depends on imagination. (This approach is also common earlier on, so it would be misleading to represent it as a distinctively eighteenth-century development. It is fair to say that in the later period there was a clearer division of labor between philosophers concerned with the imagination, and medical writers concerned with physical processes.) Imagination remains closely associated with the body and senses. But as Smith's account illustrates, it is also held to consist in the ability to conceive someone else's circumstances and feelings, and this conscious appreciation of another person's situation is widely taken to play a vital part in generating an answering affect. The workings of sympathy, as this account presents them, need not be under our control; but they are nevertheless more transparent than the projections or occult hormonal diffusions to which Teresa appeals, and because they are not so unequivocally physical, it is less clear how sympathetically-generated passions can alter the body. Instead of representing affects as corporeal phenomena capable of passing through the bodily boundary, this view makes affective transmission depend on the imagination of the recipient, and this change, so the argument suggests, is itself a repression. If this is so, what is repressed is not the knowledge *that* affects are transmitted, but the knowledge of how this occurs; what needs to be recovered is an appreciation of the passions' physical character. I'm not sure whether Teresa would agree with this diagnosis. Although she initially seems to set great store by her physicalist claims about smell, she subsequently draws back and allows that passionate exchange may depend on a variety of causal processes.[9] However, unless she opts for a physical account of transmission, it is not yet clear that anything significant gets repressed in eighteenth-century analyses of affective exchange.

A second and potentially more illuminating historical shift focuses on the relationship between comparison and sympathy. While the first of these is dominant in the foundational fantasy, and remains crucially important to a range of seventeenth-century writers, there is in eighteenth-century philosophy a move away from it, and a connected increase in the role accorded to sympathy. The tendency of humans to use comparison to sustain their sense of self is still recognized, but comes to be viewed as less powerful than before, and as more effectively offset by the operations of sympathy, which serve to blunt the sharp edges of competition and to induce feelings of benevolence. Teresa does not discuss sympathy, but if this is the shift she has in mind, what seems to get lost is, again, not an awareness of the transmission of affect as such, nor an awareness of the transmissions that are unleashed by our tendency to compare ourselves with others, but rather what she regards as a proper recognition of the psychic power and moral significance of this latter type of passionate exchange. The exhausting reiterations of the foundational fantasy are, as this elaboration of her argument suggests, marginalized and covered over by a toothless faith in the solidarity that sympathy creates. To put the point differently, an appreciation of the strength and scope of the unwanted incursions of the negative affects into the self is successfully repressed.

This interpretation of what disappears accords with Teresa's account of the eighteenth century as a period in which a concern with the passions, viewed as pacifying external forces, gives way to an interest in the sentiments—benign and sociable affections that do not need to be projected out and are easily incorporated into the self (Brennan 2004, 104–105). Read in this fashion, her analysis remains firmly grounded on her earlier, post-Freudian conception of the genesis and maintenance of the self, and encourages us to use it to rewrite the history of the affects. However, if we accept the narrative I have offered, we shall find ourselves constrained to realize that the repression with which Teresa is concerned is partly achieved by a theory about the transmission of affect—an account of the sympathy that binds people together and flows across the boundaries dividing one self from another. The suppression of an understanding of the projections through which the ego is maintained would thus fail to coincide neatly with the emergence of a conception of the strongly bounded self, and the clear lines of Teresa's argument would begin to blur. The history of the transmission of affect, we would have to conclude, is more complex and varied than her striking sketch allows, and the repression around which it revolves is not as easy to pin down as her account suggests. The historical project she proposes remains one of a sequence of immensely fruitful research programs outlined in *The Transmission of Affect*, and is already proving a fertile source of new ideas. What more fitting memorial could there be?

Notes

1. See Lorraine Daston and Katherine Park, *Wonders and the Order of Nature 1150–1750* (New York: Zone Books, 2001).

2. Nicolas Malebranche, *De la recherche de la verite*, ed. Genevieve Rodis Lewis, vol.1 of *Oeuvres Completes*, ed. Henri Gouhier (Paris: Librairie Vrin, 1972), 254.

3. Koen Vermeir, "The 'Physical Prophet' and the Powers of the Imagination. Part II. A case-study on dowsing and the naturalization of the moral (1685–1710)," *Studies in the History and Philosophy of Science* 36C, no.1 (2005): 1-24.

4. See for example, *De la recherche*, 1:208, 2:121.

5. Baruch Spinoza, *Ethics*, in *The Collected Works of Spinoza*, vol. 1, ed. Edwin Curly (Princeton: Princeton University Press, 1985), sect. 3, p. 15, p. 37.

6. *Ethics*, sect. 3, p. 40, p. 35.

7. *De la recherche*, 2:121, 2:92-3.

8. Susan James, "Sympathy and Comparison. Two Principles of Human Nature," in *Essays on Hume*, ed. M. Frasca Spada and P. Kail (Oxford: Oxford University Press, 2005).

9. I also find myself wondering at this point whether her desire to identify a physical means by which a passion can move from inside one body, through the air, and into another body, may be a manifestation of the belief that the only "real" causal processes that can change the body are physical ones, so that if the affects are to be truly embodied, they must be given a physical explanation. It is difficult to tell whether she is speaking to biologists and experimental psychologists on their own terms, or expressing a philosophical commitment of her own.

References

Brennan, Teresa. 2004. *The Transmission of Affect*. Ithaca: Cornell University Press.

Hume, David. 1978. A *Treatise of Human Nature*. L.A. Shelby Bigge, ed. 2nd Edition, revised by P.H. Nidditch. Oxford: Clarendon Press.

Smith, Adam. 1976. *The Theory of Moral Sentiments*. D.D. Raphael and A.L. Macfie, eds. Oxford: Oxford University Press.

CHAPTER SIX

Emotion, Affect, Drive

For Teresa Brennan

———————⌐∽⟨⚬⟩∾———————

Charles Shepherdson

I DELIVERED AN EARLIER VERSION of this essay in October of 2003 at a memorial symposium celebrating the life and work of Teresa Brennan. I want to express my thanks to Kelly Oliver and Liz Grosz for organizing that memorial event for Teresa Brennan, and especially for inviting me to participate. It was a privilege to be there with so many of her distinguished friends, and to have a chance not only to think about her work together, but also to address in some way her sudden departure, which came as a shock to so many of us.[1]

I

In the opening sentence of "Mourning and Melancholia," Freud speaks of "the affect of mourning" (SE 14: 243).[2] In the face of a death, the work of mourning brings with it a certain affective state. Accordingly, the word for mourning, *Trauer*, designates not only the activity of the mourner, but also the disposition or grief that accompanies it. *Trauer* is thus both the ritual activity (social or religious) that one undertakes in the face of a death, and also the state of mind (mood, disposition, affective state—*Stimmung*, in Heidegger's vocabulary) that characterizes the one who mourns.

Freud notes that the position of *melancholia* should be distinguished from that of *mourning*. When the mourner withdraws from the world, unable for a time to continue with normal life, it is the loss of the object that causes suffering. The world has become suddenly poor. This is also true for the melancholic, for whom a beloved object has likewise been lost. But in the case of the melancholic, the loss of this object is intolerable, and the object, instead of being altogether lost, is maintained within the subject, entombed within the ego itself where it continues to live, with a life that brings suffering to the subject.

This suffering is different from what we find in the case of mourning. We must therefore distinguish between the grief of the subject who mourns, a grief that I will call an emotion, for reasons that will become apparent, and the suffering of the ego in melancholia, which is perhaps something different from emotion. If Freud begins by speaking not simply of mourning, but of the "affect of mourning," it is perhaps because this affect will be a central clue to the difference that he finds in melancholia, where the ego suffers in a different way because the object remains alive within the ego. For Freud, one consequence of this difference is that the ego is split in melancholia such that one part of the ego is deprived of the object of love in a way that is similar to mourning, while the other part of the ego, the part that has identified with the lost object, exhibits a series of distinctively melancholic conditions—conditions that Freud gathers together under the heading of self-reproach. "The patient represents his ego to us as worthless, incapable of any achievement and morally despicable...He abases himself before everyone and commiserates with his own relatives for being connected with anyone so unworthy" (SE 14: 246). The melancholic exhibits "an extraordinary diminution in his self-regard, an impoverishment of his ego on a grand scale" (ibid.). This is the consequence of the internalization of the lost object, for Freud, who condenses the matter in a beautiful formulation: "In mourning it is the world that has become empty; in melancholia it is the ego itself."

Now most of the clinical literature on melancholia has taken up this feature of self-reproach, guilt, and even hatred, insofar as the splitting of the ego in melancholia allows the subject to hate in himself the object that has died and abandoned him. We have become familiar with this discussion in several contexts, but perhaps most famously in discussions of the Holocaust, the AIDS pandemic, and other events that confront us with the problem of "survivor guilt." "The shadow of the object fell upon the ego," Freud says, "and the latter could henceforth be judged by a special agency as though it were an object, a forsaken object" (SE 14: 249). We know that this special agency is taken up elsewhere by Freud in his work on the ravages of the superego, which speaks in a voice that is not the voice of the subject, but that nevertheless commands the subject in an irrevocable and terrible way.[3] Most of the secondary literature, from Melanie Klein's work on love, guilt, and reparation, to more recent work in trauma studies, has taken up this reference to guilt in the melancholic's relation to death. One might think, from these discussions, that the affect of mourning—what I called the emotion of grief—is matched by an affect of melancholia, such as guilt or self-loathing or moral masochism. The recent turn in cultural studies to the problem of "emotion" might well follow the path of these commentaries, in which the terms "emotion" and "affect" are used interchangeably.[4] But perhaps mourning and melancholia are not situated at the same level as two different emotional states, which we can call "grief" or "sorrow" on the one hand, and "guilt" or "self-reproach" on the other. Perhaps there is a more fundamental difference, one that obliges us to distinguish, not between two emotional states, but more fundamentally between *an emotion and an affect*.

To be sure, Freud did not make this distinction in his technical vocabulary, but one can see it emerge in his thinking, not only in this text, but across the entire course of his work. To put things in a somewhat formulaic way, we can say that affect and emotion are distinguished in the same way as a *charge of energy* is distinguished from an articulated and meaningful *relation to the other*. In Freud, particularly in the early theory of anxiety, this is expressed in the distinction between "accumulated tension" and "sexual desire," a distinction which is far more complex and murky than the commentaries have suggested.[5] But from this first approximation, in this case, a division between anxiety and desire, the issue is clear enough; in Lacan's terminology, it is a question of the border between the real and the symbolic. An affect presents us with a charge of jouissance and a dimension of bodily suffering which is quite distinct from an emotion, which entails, to be sure, a strong bodily dimension, but which maintains a symbolic link. It is precisely this link that is compromised in the case of melancholia where we find a symbolic rupture that leaves the subject vulnerable to the intrusion of a voice that forces the subject to expend his hatred on himself and to remain absent and withdrawn from the process of mourning (and all the sociality it entails), incapacitated by the jouissance of a symptom that we call self-reproach, in contrast to the mourner who feels grief in connection with others who likewise grieve.[6]

We can take an additional step at this point. The charge of jouissance that we see in the melancholic's self-castigation belongs to the register of the drive and sexuality, while the grief of the mourner belongs to the register of the ego and its pleasure and pain, and thus presents us with a very different form of suffering. Thus, when Lacan, speaking of the superego, says that "the voice of the Other should be considered an essential object," he means that the voice as an object of the drive is something peculiar, something that falls outside the order of speech and communal memory. The voice, then, cannot be reduced to the symbolic order any more than the gaze can be reduced to the field of the imaginary (Lacan 1990, 87). Contrary to appearance, the melancholic's relation to the voice is not a symbolic phenomenon, like the cry of mourning in which even the most elemental wailing is understood as a form of speech or address, but is a matter of jouissance and the drive. This means that the self-reproach of the melancholic is not in fact an "emotion," properly speaking, but is rather what we must call an affect, a charge of energy that signals the presence of the object, which Lacan calls the object voice.

Freud himself points out that this is really a question about libido. In mourning, the subject's libido withdraws from the world, and the subject is preoccupied with grief, for a time, given over to the labor of mourning, until the libido finds a way back to another object. But in melancholia, Freud says, the libido does not simply withdraw, but is identified with the object, and remains attached to that object, which is buried within the ego. It is *that portion of the libido*, Freud says, identified with the lost object, which is then able to turn on the ego with the vengeance of self-reproach. The voice that accuses and incriminates the subject, on this account, is nothing other than a discharge of libido, in contrast with the voice of the mourner, whose discourse and feeling of grief are a form of address to the other who is gone. How are we to understand the border that separates this dimension of affective petrification from the domain of emotional life, in which the relation to the other remains open?[7] What is the relation between the symbolic and the real of jouissance, and how might it lead us to distinguish between affect and emotion more clearly?

Let us note that this peculiar manifestation of the voice, understood as the mark of a rupture in the fabric of the symbolic order, also amounts to a retreat of the subject, a sort of fading, as Lacan suggests in *Television* when he notes that the "who" that is suddenly incarnated here in this moment of melancholic capitulation, cannot be directly identified with the subject. On the contrary, the voice in melancholia poses the question, "who speaks?," and points to an internal differentiation, a geography of the subject that demands further elaboration, much as Freud did by suggesting that the ego is split in melancholia. In Lacan's words:

> The voice of the Other should be considered an essential object . . . Its manifestations should be followed, as much in the realm of psychosis as at that extremity of normal functioning in the formation of the superego . . . Here we can no longer elude the question: beyond he who speaks in the place of the Other, and who is the subject, what is it whose voice, each time he speaks, the subject takes? (Lacan 1990, 87)

In short, it is not only the spectacular instances of psychotic delusion that reveal the ravaging function of the voice, as Freud already revealed in his accounts of paranoia, but also the more familiar labyrinths of "normal functioning" which likewise testify to the intrusion of the superego in its malicious and punishing form, and the collapse of the subject that ensues.

II

In order to clarify the status of the voice, not in relation to the usual rubric of paranoia, but in relation to the question of mourning, let us consider briefly the case of Hamlet. Hamlet cannot mourn. His famous incapacity to act, and the long temporal suspension of his desire, the "madness" that dominates the play—feigned, to be sure, but also quite real—can be read as a failure of mourning, whereby his status as a subject is compromised. But let us not conclude too quickly that this melancholic state is merely a personal characteristic or a sign of his unique individual subjectivity.

As Brennan insisted over many years, we should not be too quick to think of affect as a "personal" trait, confined to the autonomous ego. If Hamlet cannot mourn, this is not an internal psychological failure. It is the transmission of a parental structure: his mother, Gertrude, made no effort to symbolize the death of her husband, but took the funeral meats directly to the wedding ceremony, before they were even cold. His father, was struck down by poison, as Shakespeare carefully notes, before he was able to register any illness, or establish any relation to his own death—the very point which also prevents Hamlet from killing Claudius when the latter, by contrast, has just finished preparing his soul for the afterlife. As a result of this double breach in his relation to death the father returns to haunt the memory of his son to ask for a symbolization where none was given. "Remember me," says the ghost, and Hamlet's own subjectivity is all but wiped away:

> Remember thee!
> Yea, from the very table of my memory
> I'll wipe away all trivial and fond records
> All saws of books, all forms, all pressures past
> That youth and observation copied there
> *And thy commandment all alone shall live*
> *within the book and volume of my brain* (I.v. 772–78)

What are the consequences for Hamlet? According to Lacan, Hamlet abuses Ophelia, mistreats her and proves unable to recognize her, because the shadow of his father has fallen over him.[8] Love is compromised by a failure of mourning, a failure that will exact its toll. Hamlet's own ego, Lacan tells us, now contains the paternal object which has not been properly buried. As a result, his libidinal investment is withdrawn from the world, not for a publicly or commonly designated time in which mourning might take place, but withdrawn in accordance with another time, a period of suspended animation, filled with doubt, hesitation, and almost suicidal self-incrimination. At the limit of symbolic belonging, and filled with a jouissance that is not his own, suspended on the borders of the decision "to be or not to be," Hamlet is lost in melancholia.

In melancholy, Freud says, the shadow of the object has fallen across the ego. What this means is that the normal process of mourning, whereby the loss of the object is symbolized, fails to take place and the lost object, in spite of its absence, remains alive, buried within the tomb of the ego itself, so that the libidinal movement to another object becomes impossible. Ophelia is abused, then, in connection with Hamlet's melancholy. Lacan tells us that Ophelia herself is not herself, for Hamlet, and is no longer recognizable by him, but is only a figure for the mother, Gertrude, whose refusal or incapacity to mourn has made her an object of scorn and contempt, which finally overflows beyond Gertrude ("Frailty, thy name is woman"), displaced by Hamlet onto the innocent girl. Ophelia's destiny, and perhaps Hamlet's to some extent, already sketches the outline of Brennan's reading of a certain formation of "femininity," which is not only characterized by the reception of historical fallout such as this—what Brennan thematizes as the "transmission of affect"—but which reaches its culmination in Ophelia's suicide, itself no longer intelligible, on this account, as a merely "personal" event.

If Lacan's reading of Hamlet is in essence a reading of the destiny of desire, however, what can we say about the unfolding of Hamlet's destiny, given this initial impasse? If the relation to the paternal object, itself abandoned and unwept, indeed provokes a melancholic identification in which Hamlet's desire is compromised, and he is struck by self-reproach, guilt, and the withdrawal of libido into the tomb of an ego that is no longer even his own, but is rather the sacrificial tomb in which the object remains alive, then what can we say about Hamlet's destiny in the course of the drama? As Darian Leader has observed, Hamlet in the end finds it possible to love Ophelia again. He jumps into her grave with an agonized gesture, a genuine declaration of love that undoes all the previous deceptive subterfuge and indirection of his earlier courtly demeanor, that contrived madness in which truth was only indirectly declared, and relations with others were swamped by paranoia and deceit. How is this later moment possible? How does Hamlet pass from his melancholic state to what we can only call an act of mourning? Recall that Laertes appears mourning his sister, grieving loudly and protesting her death. He declares his love, and Hamlet sees in the other a relation to the lost object that he cannot achieve by himself. but that he finds through his alter ego, who traces out for him the path of a libidinal investment that he could not attain by himself.[9]

We may believe today that mourning is a private event, a matter of personal sorrow that isolates each of us, and, like all emotion, we must bear individually in silence, which would thus stand as the most intimate and individuated core of our experience, the least amenable to discourse, the least shared and communicable. Brennan showed us a different path. Emotion, she argued, is always exchanged, as a bodily energy that exceeds the boundaries of the ego, and indicates a primordial sociality that challenges the modern fantasy of the "autonomous ego." But if, as we have suggested, there is a difference between emotion and affect, if Freud claims that the status of the subject in mourning must be distinguished from the subject in melancholia, and if Lacan's account leads us to distinguish between desire and jouissance, how might this distinction clarify or further the work that Brennan left us?

Since Brennan made no distinction between the two, for her, affect and emotion are always social, primordially so, and cannot be adequately conceived as "personal" or "psychological" phenomena. Like Lacan, she insisted on the relation between the interiority of psychic life, and the institutional and discursive horizon in which it is formed. This is why, in *History After Lacan* (1993), she argued, against the prevailing view at that time, that Lacan's theory of subject-formation was not an isolated, structuralist, and therefore ahistorical theory (structuralism was never ahistorical in this way), but was also a theory of history. For Lacan, she argued, the contemporary experience of the ego was part of a broader theoretical and institutional development dating roughly from the seventeenth century, the scientific revolution, and the Enlightenment—what Jacques-Alain Miller, in the epigraph to Brennan's book, calls "the 'modern ego,' that is to say, the paranoic subject of scientific civilization . . . at the service of free enterprise." Her argument thus sets the analysis of Lacan in a broader theoretical and institutional horizon. She views the entire development of psychoanalysis as an emerging critique of the larger historical movement in which proper or normal subjectivity comes to be defined in terms of its capacity for individual, autonomous, self-conscious agency; and she argues that this model in turn must be understood against the background of scientific and economic rationality after the Renaissance.

Brennan thereby opened important lines of communication between Lacan and other thinkers, where an oppositional reception had quite mistakenly separated Lacanian psychoanalysis from other historical, economic and philosophical modes of thought—purportedly "historical" thinkers. In this way, Brennan forged several large and sweeping alliances between Lacan and other thinkers, particularly Marx, Heidegger and feminist theorists, who in different ways had launched a similar critique of the "subject" of modernity, understood as an autonomous, productive subject of representation constructed on a masculine model of scientific rationality. That this model was a fantasy and did not provide an accurate account of our social and psychic life—that it was part of what she called "the ego's era," which concealed the primordially intersubjective dimension of our affective experience, and obliged the outcast, the disenfranchised, and the unrecognized to bear the burden of hostility, aggression or self-doubt that "proper" subjects could not tolerate within themselves—was all part of the argument in *History After Lacan*, which claimed that the modern ego could not have arisen without the institutional support of capital, class struggle, and private property. Without entering into the details of her argument, let us simply say here that she understood very well the profoundly intersubjective and even socio-economic foundation of human affectivity, the contemporary forms of which she linked, in *History After Lacan*, to the development of subjectivity in post-Enlightenment European thought.

Since Brennan was also one of the rare Marxist feminists to take psychoanalysis seriously, and since the details of Freudian thought were crucial to *The Interpretation of the Flesh*, let us pay our respects to the internal details of our psychoanalytic itinerary a little longer. For Brennan did not distinguish between affect and emotion, and we are suggesting that such a distinction would have clarified the territory that she herself wished to explore.

III

We have said that the melancholic's self-castigation belongs to the register of the drive and sexuality, while the grief of the mourner belongs to the register of the ego and its pleasure and pain. In his text on "The Instincts and Their Vicissitudes," which was written the same year as the text on mourning, Freud himself makes the same observation about the difference between the ego and the drive. (Kalpana Seshadri-Crooks raises this issue with her remarks on love in her elegant and moving chapter in this volume.) Freud tells us, in effect, that an emotion is situated at the level of the ego and its relations to others, whereas the sexual instincts—*Triebe*, which Freud's English translation renders as "instincts," but which Lacanians translate as "drives"—have a different sort of object Abraham calls this a "partial object" which Lacan develops in terms of the "object a."[10] When it comes to the instinct and its satisfaction, Freud says:

> We might at a pinch say of an instinct that it "loves" the objects towards which it strives for purposes of satisfaction; but to say that an instinct "hates" an object strikes us as odd. Thus we become aware that the attitudes of love and hate cannot be made use of for the relations of instincts to their objects, but are reserved for the relations of the total ego to objects. (SE 14:137)

What this means is that the emotions of love and hate can be situated at the level of the ego's relation to its objects, such as the other who is gone, but that the drive's relation to its object is not really describable in terms of emotions like love and hate, which have a symbolically elaborated place. The energy of the drive and its peculiar "satisfaction" must therefore be distinguished from the "disposition" of the ego that we see in the emotions of love and hate.

One might object that Freud himself does not distinguish between affect and emotion. In fact, his vocabulary does not seem to support such a distinction at first glance. He speaks of the "affect of mourning," where we are claiming that mourning entails "emotion," and that "affect," properly speaking, should be reserved for the distinctive form of suffering that we find in melancholia. Moreover, we have just spoken of the "guilt" of the melancholic, which, like the "grief" of the mourner, must surely be regarded as an "emotion" in some sense. No doubt. It is clear that "emotion" may arise in both mourning and melancholia, and it cannot be a matter of simply separating two domains into dyadic and opposite camps (emotion and affect, language and the body, mourning and melancholia—so many familiar tropes of tedious opposition). The relation between the symbolic and the real is not as simple as this. The point is not to claim, therefore, that melancholia has no relation to emotion, or even, to take the opposite view, that there is no difference between mourning and melancholia, and that mourning is already the impossibility of mourning, and is already melancholic in its essence. The point is rather to recognize the distinctive position of the subject in each case, and the intricacy of the morphology Freud points to—a matter that requires both philosophical and clinical precision. If Freud seems at first glance to use a looser vocabulary, without demanding a division between affect and emotion, as though "grief" and "guilt" were both at the same level, such that mourning and melancholia were both "emotional states," a closer look complicates the matter. For when Freud notes that the ego is distinctively split in melancholia, he observes not only that *the ego feels guilt*, and that we are indeed dealing with an emotional register in some degree, but also that *some other agency takes satisfaction* in punishing the ego, depriving it of any access to life, as if the melancholic were buried in a tomb. Freud's elaboration of this point suggests that we are faced with an important difference, such that, while the ego is mortified with *a feeling* of guilt, this other agency appears under the heading of "satisfaction"; that is to say, as a *discharge of energy*, the punishing discharge of the superego, which, from another scene or another place, takes its own satisfaction in the ego's suffering. This is what Freud means by claiming that there is a difference between the pleasure and pain of the ego, and the sexual satisfaction of the drive. Here again, the drive entails a particular mode of enjoyment (*jouissance*), an affective discharge that lies outside the sphere of the ego, which for its part is taken up with the "emotions" of guilt or self-castigation. This dimension of obscure and punishing jouissance, in which the position of the subject is compromised, is what distinguishes the "guilt" of the melancholic from the "grief" of the subject who mourns. *Trauer* or "grief," as the emotion that characterizes mourning, would thus be the alternative to the affective distribution of melancholia, with its paralyzing force that we sometimes call "guilt" or "self-hatred," that comes closer to the satisfaction of the drive.

If I begin by suggesting that the difference between mourning and melancholia can be understood more clearly if we distinguish between emotion and affect, and if I suggest that the charge of jouissance that Freud sees in the melancholic's self-reproach must be understood as an affect, and distinguished from the emotions of love and hate that characterize the mourner's relation to the lost object, this is partly because it raises a clinical question: How do we pass from melancholia to mourning? How is the jouissance of the symptom of self-reproach, in which the subject's own voice is lost, to be replaced by a genuine emotion of mourning? What allows the painful satisfaction that appears in the subject's self-incrimination, and all its affective discharge, to be transformed into a symbolic elaboration wherein the object can finally be lost, detached from the tomb of the ego and allowed to pass away?[11] How does one give up the jouissance of self-hatred, and the punishing satisfaction of the drive, and pass to the level at which the object can really be lost so that the voice of the subject can return? In Lacan's terms, we can ask how jouissance condescends to desire: "jouissance," he writes in a famous formula, "must be refused, so that it can be reached on the inverted ladder of the Law of desire" (Lacan 1977, 324; 1966, 827).[12] How is this transformation possible?

These questions are at the heart of a symposium such as this where we gather together not only for intellectual reasons, but also to address the sudden passing of Teresa Brennan, which motivates our being here together. We are seeking to transform the shock of her departure by speaking together about her work. From the earliest burial mounds to the most elaborate ceremonies, mourning has always confronted this task of negotiating the border between the symbolic and the real, finding a symbolic containment for the void, which is also the passage to the future. But if these questions are present for us today, it is also because they are already the very questions that lay at the heart of Brennan's own work, which traced this path for us in advance, insofar as she was deeply concerned with the transformation of affect, especially as it circulates within the body politic. Brennan showed us again and again, the destinies or "vicissitudes" ("destiny," *Schicksal*, is the term Freud uses for the title of his paper, "Triebe und Triebschicksale," "the drives and their destinies") of our affective life are diverse, and can lead either to debilitating exhaustion and passivity, or to forms of vital and productive creation in which our desires are expressed and mobilized. But how are we to clearly grasp this difference? This is where clinical and philosophical interests overlap.

Brennan showed us how affect that cannot be tolerated within the economy of the modern ego—everything that the imaginary ideal fails to contain—does not simply disappear, but is transmitted to others, who become its carriers. She argued that this burden is in turn passed down historically even to those who did not experience the original events. One thinks of traumatic memory, which allows the events of the Holocaust, slavery, or genocide, to be lived even by those who had no direct experience of the events. In this context, it becomes difficult to speak of "the subject" in an abstract way, not only because the subject is no longer simply a "personal" entity, but also because this differential inheritance within social life makes the generalized concept of "the subject" conspicuously inadequate. This is why a more precise geography, such as the one I have outlined between mourning and melancholy, in which differences appear as having genuine significance, takes on an ethical as well as a clinical significance.

The reference to trauma introduces yet another difficulty. By raising the question of "events" that were never experienced as such, but that nevertheless become part of the subject's existence, and continue to have effects, the concept of trauma obliges us to speak of "unprocessed" or even "unsymbolized" experience, which can only lead to the enigma of an experience that is never experienced, and never given an adequate place in the order of historical memory. Such is the status of the "traumatic event" in current discourses which argue that the distinctive feature of trauma—what separates it from ordinary experience—is precisely that it occurs with a shock or suddenness that prevents it from entering the ordinary classificatory schemas of mental life. The result is that the traumatic event is confined to a sort of limbo, imprinted upon the subject without becoming part of the subject's "experience," and thus unable to find its place in a memorable narrative.[13] If the trauma returns in flashbacks and nightmares, if it re-appears out of the past like a ghost, this is because the "event" of the trauma never took place, in the sense that it never came to be properly inscribed in any symbolic chain. This does not mean it simply disappeared. On the contrary, forgotten but not forgotten, it remains, and is even transmitted, but it is not handed down in the manner of ordinary historical memory. For some thinkers, the "event" of trauma, because it does not have a discursive form, can only be betrayed by efforts of narration, and can only be truly witnessed as a break in language itself. In fact, the clinical question concerning the possibility of *transforming* traumatic events, and thus having an effect upon them, depends precisely on the degree to which the limitations of ordinary narrative knowledge are acknowledged. Psychoanalysis, Lacan said, is a way of working on the real with symbolic means, but this does not mean that one can ignore the distinctive character of the real itself. Something similar emerges in trauma theory.

Speaking of Paul de Man, for example, Cathy Caruth notes that the trauma has the status of a "disruption" in language, a moment one might call "performative," meaning that instead of saying something, it acts: "Philosophy must, and yet cannot, fully integrate a dimension of language that not only shows, or represents, but acts. Designating this moment as 'fatal,' de Man associates it with death" (Caruth 1996, 87).[14]

At stake in this discussion, therefore, is another version of what we have introduced through the distinction between mourning and melancholy, namely, the limits of the symbolic order, and the need for a clearer account of those limits, which Lacan takes up especially in terms of the real and jouissance. The need for a more satisfactory account of this limit is in fact a principle reason for Brennan's interest in Lacan:

> Derrida's critique of anti-foundationalism is a critique of a self-presencing subject. I have called the fantasy foundation because I am in full agreement with this critique, as far as it goes . . . . By Derrida's account the subject is born into a play of signification, and does not found it. Against the idea of the foundational present subject is the play of difference. But the foundational fantasy, as I will describe it, requires a different kind of foundation. It requires a foundation before the foundation, a foundation which is conceived in non-subjective terms. (Brennan 1993, 16)

Brennan refers to Spinoza here, and a certain sort of naturalism, which she also calls "matter" and "flesh." The terms are not entirely worked out in this book, as she herself points out, but the thrust of the argument is to explore an alternative to what she sees as deficient (perhaps unfairly) in Derrida, Foucault, and other proponents of the "linguistic turn." Remarkably, and no doubt because of her immersion in Freud, she does not join the ranks of those who confused Lacan with a purely "linguistic" theory, whatever that might be. Rather, she sees Lacan and Freud as offering a way to think the limit of representation:

> Derrida's position, like Foucault's, stops short after uncovering the basis of the subject's illusions about itself. It does not go on to postulate an alternative source of meaning. I will challenge this by postulating a three-stage rather than a two-stage process. That is to say, in the (Derridean) two-stage process, the foundational present subject of meaning is composed of a play of difference in which there is no meaning or inherent conation [a term she takes from Spinoza]... In the three-step process, which conceives a foundation before the subjective foundation, the subject's construction of its illusory priority is both an active appropriation and a theft...the subject invests itself with the properties that animate the generative logical chain of nature. (ibid., 16–17)

If, however, we follow the path of trauma theory, or indeed that of psychoanalysis, which is not to say these are the same, since in fact there are significant divergences, and if we follow Brennan's own path with respect to her interest in the historical transmission of "forgotten" or "unrepresented" events, which nevertheless leave their marks on human experience at the level of affective existence, it is not clear that she needs the reference to a "foundation before the foundation," or even that this reference makes her argument. The decisive feature of affect, as she herself explains it, is that it always circulates, for better and worse, sometimes in the service of vitality, and sometimes as the mark of forgotten conflict, through discursive and institutional networks of power and representation. Affect itself is thus a phenomenon that does not appear in nature. It belongs to the human being as a being for whom "the time is out of joint." In this, Brennan would have agreed with Foucault and Derrida. This does not mean that we should ignore the differences between the destitute and the privileged, any more than we should pretend that mourning and melancholia are both "emotions" at the same level, where there is in fact a significant difference with respect to the possibilities of subjective life.

This is where Lacan, and in particular, the distinction between affect and emotion, would have pushed her formulations further. The real in Lacan is not a natural, prediscursive foundation which the symbolic would either approximate or betray. Correlatively, affect is not a biological energy that, if it is not symbolically contained, overflows onto its unfortunate recipients. The real is rather an effect of symbolization, and thus an abyss in the field of meaning, a product of the Other, in Lacan's language. Consequently, the real does not have the status of a natural entity, as Brennan wished in some of her more speculative and idealistic moments, but is a void introduced into being by the operation of representation. Like the "traumatic event," it cannot be confused with what one might imagine "actually happened," since its traumatic status depends upon the return, after the fact, of an event whose peculiar character consists in the fact that it never simply "took place." All the temporal problems of memory, historical time, and the organizing chains of signification must be primordial to the very possibility of "trauma," which cannot be grasped by any reference to a pre-linguistic domain.[15]

Brennan's work explored the transmission of affect in considerable detail over many years. She developed the theme of affective mobility at the level of both subjective and political life. In relation to what she called "femininity," for instance, she described a psychic position that could be assumed by anyone, but that was characterized by the assumption, on the part of a given subject, of all the excess energy that the "normal" and "masculine" ego could not contain within itself. "Affect" here was not a private or personal matter, but was understood largely as a silent or barely articulated experience of exhaustion or incapacity that was distributed unevenly in the social sphere. But "affect" in her work could also include experiences of exhilaration and vitality. She tied this alternative between life and death to political movements, which have the capacity either to function in powerful historical ways, or to lose their energy and force. If she did not distinguish between affect and emotion, or rely to any great extent on a Lacanian framework—open though she clearly was to Lacan's thinking—we might venture to suggest that such a distinction between affect and emotion, together with a sharper account of what Lacan develops under the category of jouissance, might cast some light on precisely these alternative destinies, thereby contributing to her own intellectual itinerary, and clarifying some points that remained obscure in her work.

IV

Let me therefore try to link these remarks more closely to Brennan's work on femininity as it appears in Freud's work, which she so carefullly mapped out in *The Interpretation of the Flesh*. In his early work on hysteria, we know that Freud regarded the symptom not as an organic disease, but as a somatized peculiar form of memory insofar as it was not remembered by the conscious mind, but inscribed at the level of the flesh. When Freud writes that "hysterics suffer mainly from reminiscences," he is speaking of a bodily symptom, not of reminiscence in the ordinary sense, since the mind precisely forgets what the symptom remembers. There is a disjunction between "consciousness" and "the body," even if the body is clearly not a natural phenomenon but is fully implicated in the functions of representation.

We also know that in his attempt to explain the dissolution of the symptom under hypnosis, and even later under psychoanalysis proper, Freud observed that it was not sufficient for the patient to recall the repressed memory, or simply to symbolize what had fallen outside the field of representation and landed in the body as a result. In order for the symptom to be dissolved, the repressed memory had to be recalled along with, at the same time, the affective charge that was attached to the initial traumatic event. Memory without affect is insufficient, he says. In Lacanian terms, we could say that the jouissance of the symptom will not be reached by symbolization alone. What is required is rather that speech and memory and the order of representation be mobilized in such a way as to have an effect on the affective charge that was attached to the original traumatic experience:

> For we found, to our great surprise at first, that each individual hysterical symptom immediately and permanently disappeared when we had succeeded in bringing clearly to light the memory of the event by which it was provoked *and in arousing its accompanying affect*, and when the patient had described that event in the greatest possible detail *and had put the affect into words*. Recollection without affect almost invariably produces no result. ("On the Psychical Mechanism of Hysterical Phenomena," SE 2:6, emphasis added)

In Lacanian terms, we can say that the symbolic order is not the whole truth. Despite his purportedly linguistic and structuralist orientation, it is clear that Lacan never regarded the symbolic order as a sufficient theoretical domain—not because there is also a question of the imaginary, as is so often said, but because psychoanalysis is a way of working on the real with symbolic means. Symbolization in itself is not a sufficient agenda for Lacan just as, for Freud, the memory or discourse without affect is insufficient to produce a shift at the level of the symptom. By the same token, we can say that there is no access to the pure affective charge of the trauma *without* representation, and that the real of the symptom, as it is understood in psychoanalysis, can only be approached through the detour of the symbolic order.

This relation between the symbolic and the real of jouissance was the core of Freud's work on the hysterical symptom. It is precisely this relation that led Brennan back to the problem of affect and energy in Freud. This was not as an *alternative* to the excessively linguistic or purportedly structuralist formulations of Lacan, but much rather as an effort to unfold and conceptual-ize the *relationship* between the symbolic order and "energy," or "emotion" and "affect," together with what Freud developed under the heading of the "drive," which appears on the border of language. Although "affect" and "emotion" are often used interchangeably, it should be clear that all these terms demand a more careful exposition. Psychoanalysis is a means of working on the real with symbolic means. This was already clear from Freud's early accounts of traumatic memory and the hysterical symptom, even if Freud did not use the Lacanian vocabulary. The same distinction reappears later in Freud's work.

In his article on "Repression," where we might expect Freud to place the strongest possible emphasis on the symbolic order with references to the familiar formations of the unconscious—the lapsus, the dream, free associa-tion, and all the verbalized forms of negation and denial that Freud presents as the surest sign that something unconscious is appearing in speech under the disguise of censorship, or a repudiation by the ego ("You'll think it's my mother in the dream," Freud says, "but it's not my mother"). Even here, in the midst of this account of the symbolic nature of unconscious manifestations, Freud is far more careful and precise: "In our discussion so far," he writes, "we have dealt with the repression of an instinctual representative, and by the latter we have understood an idea or group of ideas which is cathected with a definite quota of psychical energy (libido or interest) coming from an instinct" ("Repression," SE 14:152). At this point in Freud's discussion, we would seem to be concerned with a division, *within the field of representation*, between those highly cathected ideas or signifiers or "instinctual represen-tatives" which are repressed, and those which are not repressed—conscious and unconscious "ideas" or signifiers, one might say. But Freud then adds that "some other element" has to be accounted for:

Clinical observation now obliges us to divide up what we have hitherto regarded as a single entity; for it shows us that besides the idea, some other element has to be taken into account, and that this element undergoes

vicissitudes of repression which may be quite different from those undergone by the idea. For this other element of the psychical representative
the term *quota of affect* has generally been adopted. It corresponds to the
instinct insofar as the latter has become detached from the idea and finds
expression, proportionate to its quantity, in processes which are sensed as
affects. From this point on, we shall have to follow up separately what,
as the result of repression, becomes of the *idea*, and what becomes of the
instinctual energy linked to it. (ibid.)

Thus, besides the ideas which are "cathected with a definite quota of psychical energy," and either mobilized by consciousness or repressed, we must
now confront a "quota of affect," an element that is "detached from the idea,"
and given a different destiny. ("This element," Freud says, "undergoes vicissitudes of repression which may be quite different from those undergone by
the idea.")[16]
    This new division between the field of representation and the "quota of
affect" is not as simple as it might seem. We cannot simply speak of a difference between the "idea" and "energy," or the "signifier" and the "drive," as if
it were a matter of separating the "psychic" domain of representation from the
domain of "bodily" experience or "affective" energy. For one thing, it is clear
from Freud's formulation that the "psychic" domain of representation already
entails a certain appeal to "energy" or "libido." Freud thus speaks of "an idea
or group of ideas which is cathected with a definite quota of psychical energy
(libido or interest) coming from an instinct." This "new element," while it is
distinct from the "idea" or signifier, cannot be construed as a bodily experience
that would be altogether unrelated to the sphere of representation. Accordingly, Freud writes that "some other element *representing the instinct* has to be
taken into account," and he goes on to offer the following definition: "For
this other element *of the psychical representative* the term quota of affect has
generally been adopted" ("Repression," SE 14:152, emphasis added). Thus,
on the side of representation, there is energy, and on the side of affect, there
is representation.[17]
    If this development in Freud's work is serious, we cannot simply obliterate
the distinction he seeks to make, any more than we should obliterate the distinction between mourning and melancholia, or between emotion and affect.
This much is clear: instead of a simple division between the "psychic" sphere
of representation or ideas, and the "bodily" sphere of immediate presence and
natural energy, we have a more complex and tangled relation. One in which it
is still possible to differentiate, "to follow up separately," what Freud calls, in a
tentative and problematic way, the "idea" and this "other element" which has
become detached from the idea and appears as a "quota of affect" that follows
a different path and is subject to different vicissitudes. Given this peculiar

relationship of intertwining in which a difference emerges in spite of the fact that instinctual energy and representation appear on both sides, one might say that Freud seeks to isolate, not an "outside" to representation, a domain of natural immediacy or affect or emotion that no representation would touch, such as the familiar notion of "instinct," but a point *within* the domain of representation that remains essentially foreign, excluded, and impossible to present—"detached," as Freud says, from the idea or representation. Such is the relation between the symbolic and the real—the latter being understood not as a prelinguistic reality, or as an affective core that would somehow precede representation, but as an effect of the symbolic order that is nevertheless not reducible to a symbolic phenomenon. In Lacanian terms, we are concerned here with the difference between the Other and the object *a*; it is above all the theory of the drive that obliges us to acknowledge this distinction.

It is remarkable that Brennan seized on this issue more than ten years ago, at a time when everyone else was denouncing the purportedly linguistic excesses of Lacanian theory. It is even more striking that she was able to grasp this issue of energy, drive, and affect as a key to the question of femininity at a time when most Anglo-American interpreters of Lacan were focusing on the imaginary and addressing the question of femininity in terms of the supposed confinement of women to the imaginary order, whereby entry into the symbolic order was assumed to be a male or masculine privilege. Such a view allowed Lacanian theory to be quickly absorbed by the discourse of social construction in which femininity and masculinity were seen to be structured by symbolic conventions rather than by any natural foundation. On this account, the question of femininity could readily be inserted into the discourse of gender, organized by what came to be called the "cultural imaginary," and made compatible with other forms of social theory.

Femininity could thus be grasped in terms of imaginary and symbolic identifications, but in the process, psychoanalysis itself underwent a profound distortion. The question of affect was eliminated, the jouissance of the symptom could not be addressed, the clinical specificity of psychoanalysis disappeared altogether, and the question of femininity came be formulated in imaginary terms. Femininity was reduced to a relation to the mother that the symbolic "law" of culture somehow obliged the masculine subject to relinquish or transcend, and to denigrate and renounce, while the feminine subject remained confined, on this account, to the prison of the imaginary order. The very absorption of psychoanalysis into the discourse of social construction allowed psychoanalytic feminism to be integrated into more familiar and canonical forms of knowledge. The question of femininity as Freud had formulated it had simply disappeared. This is what Teresa proposed in *The Interpretation of the Flesh*. In her chapter, "The Division of Attention," she wrote "the minute the real riddle of femininity is approached, the debates digress"

(Brennan 1992, 83). "This digression can take the form of invective against the *Penisneid* of Freud's critics; or polemic against Freud's patriarchal bias" (ibid.). In either case, Brennan writes, "the logical direction of the enquiry is diverted" (ibid.).

It was her brave and quirky independence of mind, and what one might even call her lack of piety, that allowed her to propose a connection that no one else at the time had really articulated: "It is in relation to repression that Freud formulated his hydraulic metapsychology," she writes. "This hydraulic physics may seem to be a long way from . . . the riddle of femininity, but this book's argument should show that the distance between the two is not as great as it first appears" (Brennan 1992, 30). If we follow this connection, it becomes clear that, according to Brennan femininity can no longer be approached as a gender role, or as a form of social identity in the usual sense. These forms of identity are too closely bound up with the individual subject as a unit—too bound up with the imaginary ego, like the very theories of femininity that Teresa tried to challenge. It is this distinction between femininity in the psychoanalytic sense, and its misleading equivalents in social theories of gender, that Brennan sought to maintain when she wrote that "Womanhood, or the feminine (whatever that is), is not identical with femininity in Freud's sense" (ibid., x).

For Brennan, femininity is not a form of social identity, either imaginary or symbolic, but is closer to a moment, a possible modality of energy, a transformation of affect that emerges in the relation between subjects. This is why femininity can be tied to the problem of affect, energy, and the transmissibility of emotion. "We should investigate the assumption that individuals are the sole and self-contained points of origin for their emotions," she writes; and we should recognize that "emotions can cross the boundaries between individual persons" (ibid.). If, in the course of a conversation, "the hysteric assumes the rational mantle," she observes, "the dramatic and irrational emotions sometimes pass over to the previously rational interlocutor" (ibid.). "Emotions or affects can be reversed," she writes. This is why femininity cannot be understood as a form of identity that attaches to certain culturally defined gender roles in any sociological or generalized way, much less as anything that could be attached to biological sex. Instead, it should be approached as transformation of energy, a disposition, possibility or modality in the relation to the other that can be assumed or actualized by any subject at a particular moment. "Femininity was a riddle," Brennan says, "because Freud could not explain why certain drives and affects were turned against the subject in a disabling way." "Unlike many feminists," she writes, "I have no quarrel with Freud's belief that a disabling femininity exists. Where I depart from Freud is in this: he worked with a model of a human being that was energetically self-contained" (ibid.). This is a remarkable thesis, or intuition. It is all the more remarkable that, in 1992, she could say that "the riddle of femininity will be clarified after the matter of the drives is discussed" (ibid., 35). The question of the drive is still almost never discussed, even when energy and affect are mentioned, as they are increasingly today.

If the question of the drive tends to be avoided even when energy and affect are addressed, then this is another manifestation of that diversion or digression in which psychoanalysis is avoided in favor of more familiar forms of knowledge. Teresa's remark, "the riddle of femininity will be clarified after the matter of the drives is discussed" stands before us still, as a challenge and a provocation.

Notes

1. These remarks are occasional and are not developed in the way that a normal academic paper would be developed. I have left untouched a few offhand remarks concerning the occasion of the gathering, namely Teresa's unexpected death. I have not developed many of the engagements that a proper exposition would require—above all (1) the challenge posed to the very possibility of a distinction between mourning and melancholia, by Jacques Derrida; (2) the work of Maria Torok and Nicholas Abraham; and (3) more recent work in trauma theory.

2. Sigmund Freud, "Mourning and Melancholia," *The Standard Edition of the Complete Psychological Works of Sigmund Freud*, trans. and ed. James Strachey et. al. (London: The Hogarth Press, 1953), volume 14. Henceforth references to Freud will appear in the text by volume and page number.

3. In *Group Psychology and the Analysis of the Ego* (a text written at roughly the same time as the text on mourning), Freud describes what happens to the subjects who form a bond in which ordinary social belonging—what we might call the operation of the symbolic domain—is suspended in favor of a "group" formation. Absorbed into the "group" (such as the army or the church, Freud says), such subjects experience a loss of autonomy, together with a suspension of the usual functioning of moral conscience. They allow themselves to perform the most degrading or brutally violent acts, under the guidance of a "leader" who functions, according to Freud, not in accordance with the laws of conscience, but in submission to an external authority. This has a peculiarly disastrous and punishing effect, insofar as it suspends the autonomy of the subject, who submits to an external authority. This, Freud argues, provides the model for an elaboration of the superego itself, and manifests a discordance between the superego and the law which has occupied Lacanian theory in recent years.

4. See, for example, Richard Wollheim, *On the Emotions* (New Haven: Yale University Press, 1999); Martha Nussbaum, *Upheavals of Thought: The Intelligence*

of Emotions (Cambridge: Cambridge University Press, 2001); Rei Terada, *Feeling in Theory: Emotion after the Death of the Subject* (Cambridge: Harvard University Press, 2001); and Charles Altieri, *Particulars of Rapture: An Esthetics of the Affects* (Ithaca: Cornell University Press, 2003). There are countless other neurobiological or "evolutionary psychology" texts that explain the relation between emotion and culture.

5. See Charles Shepherdson, "Foreword" to Roberto Harari, *Lacan's Seminar on Anxiety: An Introduction*, trans. Jane C. Lamb-Ruiz (New York: Other Press, 2001), pp. ix–lxxix.

6. In *Being and Time*, Heidegger distinguishes, between the "call of conscience" and the irruption of "guilt," the latter understood as a modality in which the subject falls away from itself into anonymity. What "subject" is posited in the emergence of guilt, as opposed to the subject of the call? Psychoanalysis might have allowed this distinction to be developed with greater efficacy, had Heidegger been less phobic in this regard.

7. These issues are developed by Lacan especially in his unpublished seminar on anxiety, *Seminar* X. See Roberto Harari, *Lacan's Seminar on "Anxiety": An Introduction*, trans. Jane C. Lamb-Ruiz (New York: Other Press, 2001), pp. ix–lxii.

8. For some English excerpts of Lacan's seminar on Hamlet, "Desire and its Interpretation," see *Literature and Psychoanalysis*, ed. Shoshana Felman (Baltimore: Johns Hopkins University Press, 1980).

9. Darian Leader, "Some Thoughts on Mourning and Melancholia," *Journal for Lacanian Studies*, vol. 1, number 1 (2003), 4–37.

10. Jacques-Alain Miller has noted that Lacan initially took his conception of the "object a" from Karl Abraham's account of the object of the drive (or, in the English of the Standard Edition, the "instinct"). "Where does the object *a* come from in Lacan? It comes from the partial object of Karl Abraham." ("Extimité," 85). I discuss this point at greater length in *The Epoch of the Body* (Stanford: Stanford University Press, forthcoming).

11. Literary examples of melancholia are numerous, and an entire tradition was constructed under the sign of Saturn. Let us only recall here the opening lines of Chaucer's "Book of the Dutchess," which are spoken by a man afflicted with a great sickness, who can neither love nor hate, who keeps track of nothing, and wonders how he is able to remain alive:

> I have gret wonder, be this lyght,
>
> How that I lyve, for day ne nyght
>
> I may nat slepe wel nygh noght;
>
> I have so many an ydel thought,
>
> Purely for defaute of slep,
>
> That, by my trouthe, I take no kep
>
> Of nothing, how hyt cometh or gooth,
>
> Ne me nys nothyng leef nor looth.

Al is ylyche good to me—

Joye or sorrow, wherso hyt be—

For I have felynge in nothing (1–11)

12. Jacques Lacan, "The Subversion of the Subject and the Dialectic of Desire," in *Ecrits: A Selection*, trans. Alan Sheridan (New York: Norton, 1977), p. 324; see *Écrits* (Paris: Seuil, 1966), p. 827.

13. See Bessel van der Kolk, "The Intrusive Past: The Flexibility of Memory and the Engraving of Trauma," in *Trauma: Explorations in Memory*, ed. Cathy Caruth (Baltimore: Johns Hopkins University Press, 1995), pp. 158–182.

14. See Cathy Caruth, *Unclaimed Experience: Trauma, Narrative and History* (Baltimore: Johns Hopkins University Press, 1996), p. 87.

15. I have discussed two possible readings of the "real" in more detail in "The Intimate Alterity of the Real," *Postmodern Culture*, vol. 6, no. 3 (May 1996).

16. Here, I elaborate on some remarks already made in "The Elements of the Drive," *Umbr(a): A Journal of the Unconscious*, no. 1 (1997), 131–45.

17. For further discussion of this passage see André Green, *The Fabric of Affect in the Psychoanalytic Discourse*, trans. Alan Sheridan (New York: Routledge, 1999).

References

Brennan, Teresa. 1993. *History After Lacan*. London: Routledge.

———1992. *The Interpretation of the Flesh: Freud and Femininity*. London: Routledge.

Freud, Sigmund. 1953. *The Standard Edition of the Complete Psychological Works of Sigmund Freud*. Ed. and trans., James Strachey, et. al. London: The Hogarth Press.

Lacan, Jacques. 1990. *Television: A Challenge to the Psychoanalytic Establishment*. Ed., Joan Copjec, trans. Denis Hollier, Rosalind Krauss, and Annette Michaelson. New York: Norton.

———1977. "The Subversion of the Subject and the Dialectic of Desire," in *Ecrits: A Selection*. Trans., Alan Sheridan. New York: Norton, 1977.

———1966. *Écrits*. Paris: Seuil.

CHAPTER SEVEN

After Teresa Brennan

———— ⌖ ————

Kalpana Rahita Seshadri

IN THE SPRING OF 2000, Teresa sent me her manuscript, *The Transmission of Affect*[1] and asked me to respond to it. This followed on a series of exchanges we had at first about the concept of race as a fictional device within the sociology of medicine, which then led to other related issues. Teresa had proposed that we work on an essay together, maybe even a book, on race and intelligence. She was riveted by the debates over Herrnstein and Murray's controversial some would say noxious, study of intelligence and race in America, *The Bell Curve*. Teresa suggested that we launch a different kind of attack on Herrnstein and Murray that would not offer a refutation, but would begin by accepting their findings.

Rather than focusing, as others had done, on their manipulation of statistics and questionable epistemological assumptions, Teresa wanted to make the argument that IQ variants could be directly traced to environmental and material factors. If children of certain ethnic groups perform less well in cognitive aptitude tests, we could show that this was because of their inadequate or unequal access to resources that aid in cognitive development, such as environmental and psychical factors that condition the subject's place in the world, as well as to material factors such as nutrition, schooling, parenting, health care, and pre-natal care.

For those of us who are familiar with Teresa's work, this mode of analysis, what we may term as a social biologism, is her signal achievement—the interrogation of the nature/nurture binary to demonstrate the intricate ways in which social, material, and environmental factors incarnate the flesh and produce the biological.

Though I am very much in sympathy with Teresa's brand of constructionism, when it came to actual collaboration, I found it a hard act to follow, as, it required a mode of interdisciplinary study and forms of belief, about the good, or about health, for instance, that were beyond me. More precisely, to do good

Brennanian work, requires that one be able to translate sociological analyses into tools for ethical and political argumentation based on normative judgments about the social. I also found that it requires a great deal of philosophical muscle to utilize the blunt statistical instruments of sociology to excavate the subtler layers of identity production. To be honest, I found my stamina and optimism duly waning. I was also dead set against granting anything to Herrnstein and Murray because it seemed too much like a capitulation.

For me, the very concept of race is founded and implicated in a pernicious logic of human differentiation and ranking. It was within the context of my withdrawal from the essay project, and gradual flagging of collaborative possibilities that she asked me to read her manuscript.

I am several months late with my response, but I share it with you now in this volume not because I feel a sense of unfulfilled obligation and yearn for closure, though the denial is no doubt symptomatic, but because handling the manuscript with its typographical errors and pagination mistakes positions me in a time before closure, before the book was complete, and revives for me a Teresa who is still writing, revising, thinking and arguing.

It was an inexplicable pleasure to work with the manuscript. The errors took on an unexpected affect, not that of a veiling over or of forgetting, but they revealed a materiality and a liveliness, whose loss we all collectively mourn.

———⚭———

Dear Teresa:

Your bulky manuscript arrived by Fed Ex and I have finally finished reading it with great interest and pleasure. My grasp of your concepts is no doubt tenuous, but for what it's worth, I thought I would take up your invitation to share some observations and moments of coalescence with my own ongoing work on otherness.

There are several surprising and unsettling propositions in your work, which I found a bit baffling at first, until I came to appreciate and recognize them for what they were. The work as a whole is a significant intervention into fundamental psychoanalytic concepts that I, with my propensity for textual fidelity, have accepted unquestioningly. Your overall argument that affects are intersubjective, that they are not confined to the skin boundaries of a subject, but are transmitted to others causing concrete bio-symptomatic effects seems wholly reasonable to me. I can offer as an example the physical nausea I experience every time I see the US flag with "Fear This" inscribed below, or the distraught laughter I must perforce suppress when I hear solemn pronouncements about Iraq's cache of WMDs.

The affects you speak of are not necessarily caused by words or politics, but by ego judgments and projective identifications. If I feel depressed, I transmit my gloom to you; you receive it and turn it into anger. Consequently you suffer from dyspepsia or heartburn and, while pharmaceutical companies celebrate, the vicious circle continues. I do have a question about the way in which you locate language in this process of inter-subjective transmission, but more of that later. I will also come back to your sense that contemporary modern society refutes the transmissibility of affects, that the struggle with one's passions, a praxis enshrined in several religious traditions including Christianity, has been relegated to the unconscious due to social paranoia. But first, here are some significant moments in your book that made me pause and reflect.

One of the most stunning aspects of this book, which I feel will and should have far reaching implications, is your revision of the psychoanalytic theory of affects. Throughout this manuscript, you suggest that affects are not merely signals of an imminent situation, such as anxiety as a signal to trauma, or joy as a signal to some sort of satisfaction; but that they are themselves that which penetrate the psyche and get assimilated by the body—affects, you suggest are perhaps chemical changes in the body that are transmitted atmospherically to others through smell, subtle rhythmic vibrations, and waves such as tension. They are basically "disorders of energy" causing empirically observable diseases such as Attention Deficit Hyperactivity Disorder, Chronic Fatigue Syndrome, Fibromyalgia, Depression, etc. So, the notion here is that affects are not merely accompanying signals, the heralding trumpets of external forces, but are themselves forces "material physiological things" (Brennan MS, 8) that are productive of certain effects such as trauma or satisfaction.

For Freud, affects are not transmitted, they are the transmitters—"processes of discharge," and very unreliable ones at that, of unconscious ideas and thoughts ("The Unconcious," 1963). Affect in psychoanalysis, as I've always understood it, is largely vehicular, empty of content. It is primarily a conduit of communication about repressed, inadmissible ideas, into the conscious mind. It may be kept from developing fully, as in melancholia, which is the function of repression. It can also be utterly transformed as in homophobia or racism where a particular idea, such as sexual desire, may be transformed and perceived as a feeling of hatred or disgust. Whereas in your theory, you suggest that affects are content laden and can be equated with the seven deadly sins.

Once you identify affect as an intrinsic aspect of the drive, rather than the transformation of the drive into an affect grasped by the conscious system, then it is also surprisingly subject to repression. Freud, speaks of the inevitable "looseness of phraseology" when we refer to an "unconscious or a repressed instinctual impulse" (Freud 1963, 126), but insists that what is repressed is always the idea, though its accompanying affect may be hindered from developing. Thus, when the repression is lifted we may well also speak of the release of unconscious affects that are but "potential dispositions." Freud however is quite categorical that "there are no unconscious affects in the sense in which there are unconscious ideas" (ibid., 127). It is a significant and thought provoking departure then to insist as you do that thoughts or ideas do not necessarily precede affect, and that "one may well say that the affects evoke the thoughts . . . [that] the affects may at least in some instances find thoughts that suit them, not the other way around" (Brennan MS, 10).

Your theory is even more radical than just claiming content for affect. You suggest that affect, can originate in the other and can lodge in the subject "independent of the individual experiencing them" (ibid., 17). In other words, affects are largely targeted projections that find their mark. Exactly how intentionality, conscious or unconscious, functions in transmission, and whether this should or could affect our ethical considerations are topics that I would like to see explored further.

You have been one of the most insistent and persuasive critics of the fantasy of human autonomy. In *History After Lacan*, you elaborate notions of individual autonomy as a foundational fantasy. In this work, you utilize that concept to speak of: the child's repudiation of its dependence on the mother or caregiver, the nexus of compensatory mechanisms that accompany this repudiation, and the production of the fantasy of total autonomy and sovereignty. In the scenario of the foundational fantasy, the child not only projects its passivity onto the mother, but it hallucinates instantaneity (Brennan MS, 65) and is forced to repress the unpleasure that follows from the mother's real absence. What gets repressed here is the hallucination itself and the affect of disappointment, anger, et cetera, which contribute to the formation of symptoms. The aim of psychoanalysis then is to reconnect the idea with its affect: "reconnecting thought and affect is integral to discerning the transmission of affect" (ibid., 226).

Once again, the affect is not the envelope that wraps or warps the kernel of thought—but it is the kernel itself, and the thought or the sense of autonomy, is its package. That which is usually outside becomes the true inside. This is the key feminist moment in this book insofar as the interrogation and detonation of the inside/outside, appearance/essence, private/public oppositions are central to feminist practice.

Where the foundational fantasy is concerned, there is a strange and interesting departure in this new work, and it has to do with the way in which you speak of the *function* of affects. Affects, you suggest are themselves forms of egoic, comparative judgments that one makes about an object. When one feels envy, anger, deprivation or self pity, one is adopting a judgmental stance towards the object. The key problem here, as I understand you to be stating it, is the subject/object distinction itself and the calcification of that boundary by and through the transmission of negative affects. In chapter five, you speak of the manner in which

> The illusion of self-containment is purchased at the price of dumping nega-tive affects on that other . . . By means of this projection, one believes one-self detached from him or her, when one is in fact propelling forth an affect which he will experience as rejection or hurt, unless he has shielded himself against these affects by a similar negative propulsion, a passionate judgment of his own. (Brennan MS, 248).

To halt this vicious cycle, you propose that discernment and feelings are necessary. "Discernment, in the affective world, functions best when it is able to be alert to the moment of fear of anxiety or grief or other sense of loss which permits the negative affect to gain a hold" (ibid., 249). In other words, the person receiving the negative affect, the dumpee, to use your terminol-ogy, must practice a code of detachment, and exercise his/her "finer feelings," and refuse to be swayed by the affects being transmitted. Here, you adduce religious injunctions, virtues and pre-modern acts of courtesy as discernment promoting codes. The promotion of virtue and courtesy is in itself no doubt startling. The real surprise, however, is in the idea that the person engaged in specific inter-subjective activity, the one who slaps the cheek of the other, transmitting affect and dumping on the other, is securing his/her sense of self-containment, whereas the discerning receiver who turns the other cheek, who maintains imperviousness to the affect through the constraining or prohibi-tory practices of courtesy, detachment, and virtue, is the truly inter-subjective person, one who recognizes and values his/her dependence upon the other. I find this paradoxical because it goes against an entire matrix of debate—on one hand a certain common sense attitude to dumping, and on the other the psychoanalytic rejoinder to that common sense.

The common sense view is that the person who exhibits emotion of any kind is seen to have "lost control" whereas the one who maintains a certain butler-like stoicism even in the face of personal tragedy or abuse—a stiff upper lip—is perceived as being able to master himself, to govern his emotions. Psy-choanalysis holds such common sense responsible for inducing pathological symptoms in the courteous subject. Its theory of repression and denial derives from the perception of a dialectical relation between inhibiting social norms and conventions and libidinal desires and drives.

The figure of discernment often embodied in class terms as the English aristocrat or his butler, raises some troubling questions, questions that for instance Kazuo Ishiguro in his luminous novel *The Remains of the Day* delin-eates with great human care and tenderness. I am not thinking of emotional temperatures here, being warm or cold, nor am I particularly worried about the effects of prohibiting expression of emotions per se. What I am struggling to grasp is the theoretical consequence of the notion that the person who is actually touching, stirring the other with his/her negative emotions, is in your view the one laboring under the fantasy of self-containment. What then is inter-subjectivity and how is discernment in the subject constituted? What is its relation to the other? Is this discerning subject possible outside a frame of subject-object binary?

To push these issues a little further, I would like to look at the way in which drive theory underwrites your argument about negative affects and dumping. The gist of the relation between affects and drive is available in chapter two. You write: "for while there is a difference between the notion of affect and the idea of the drives, the two are intimately connected. The drive propels the affect; it is in large part the stuff out of which the affect is made" (Brennan MS, 59). Later in the manuscript, you valorize the life drive as a liberating and inherently inter-subjective force. I am willing to maintain the opposition between the so-called life drive and the death drive, contra Lacan who says that ultimately all drives are death drives,[2] and also distinguishes life and the body. But setting aside Lacanian theory, we nevertheless cannot ignore the functionality of these drives.

The so-called life drive, which Freud proposes in *Beyond the Pleasure Principle* (1920) as a revision to his earlier opposition in *An Outline of Psycho-Analysis* (1910) between the ego and libidinal or sexual drives, is self-preserving and quintessentially defensive. What alters in the later theory is that the ego instincts are also perceived as having a sexual component. But the erotism of the life instincts is turned not towards the ego, as in sadism and masochism, but towards the preservation of the species through the building of larger unities. The death drive to which the life drive is opposed is to be understood as a transgression of the life or sexual instinct's orientation towards coalescence and identity. The life drives are implicated in the production of increasingly organized forms, and consequently in the widening of the subject/object distinction—the organism versus the environment. The negative death drive on the other hand functions to destroy not only the process of differentiation through unity and identity endemic to the life instincts, but it exposes the subject/object distinction as a fantasy. The so-called life drive then is nothing but a screen for death. Lacan therefore elaborates on Freud's expressed horror for the religious injunction to "love thy neighbor as thyself."

In his *Ethics of Psychoanalysis*, Seminar VII, Lacan speaks of the *resistance* to the commandment as a way of avoiding the *jouissance*—the murderous death drive inherent in the constitution of one's subjectivity. To love one's neighbor as oneself would be to access a violence, an aggressivity, that is screened by altruism and normalizing notions of happiness. According to Lacan, in Freud's horror at the commandment to love one's neighbor:

> We see evoked the presence of that fundamental evil which dwells within
> this neighbor. But if that is the case, then it also dwells within me. And what
> is more of a neighbor to me than this heart within which is that of my jouis-
> sance and which I don't dare go near? For as soon as I go near it . . . there
> rises up the unfathomable aggressivity from which I flee. (Lacan 1992, 186)

Lacan goes on to say that the reason we resist the commandment is because
we wish not to

> assault the image of the other, because it was the image on which we were
> formed as an ego . . . We are, in effect, at one with everything that depends
> on the image of the other as our fellow man, on the similarity we have to our
> ego to everything that situates us in the imaginary register. (ibid., 196–197)

The true practice of the virtue of neighborliness then would entail destroying
the boundaries separating the subject from the other. For what really drives us
as subjects who are constituted through a splitting, is the destructive energy
of jouissance, a desire ultimately to mutilate ourselves. The constitutive splitting of the subject, its irreducible negativity, prevents it always from being
totally subject to the benign life drive. The life drive is after all about unity,
cohesion, and the maintenance of identity. But above all, valorizing it over
the death drive requires that we aim towards a totalization of human drives,
and such an aim militates against the incompletion, the splitting that is con-
nate with the subject. However much the subject may try to heed the pulsion
of the life instinct, which presents itself as life affirming and unifying, the
inherent negativity of the subject, its "infancy," if I may borrow a term from
Giorgio Agamben, prevails. It is this negativity that, paradoxically, is generative of sociality. It makes antagonism in the most productive sense possible—
a social antagonism that can translate into political struggle. Anticolonial
struggles, labor struggles and the struggle for civil rights are all predicated on a
core capacity to react against and destroy oppression. Consider for a moment
that astonishing passage in Frantz Fanon's *The Wretched of the Earth*, where he
valorizes the affect of violence and the death drive:

> The settler keeps alive in the native an anger which he deprives of outlet;
> the native is trapped in the tight links of the chains of colonialism. But we
> have seen that inwardly the settler can only achieve a pseudo petrification.
> The native's muscular tension finds outlet regularly in bloodthirsty explo-
> sions—in tribal warfare, in feuds between septs, and in quarrels between
> individuals . . . Thus collective autodestruction in a very concrete form is
> one of the ways in which the native's muscular tension is set free. All these
> patterns of conduct are those of the death reflex when faced with danger, a
> suicidal behavior which proves to the settler . . . that these men are not
> reasonable human beings. (Fanon 1963, 54)

The core of anticolonial struggle is impelled by the death drive (loving your neighbor as yourself) in that colonial violence brings the native face to face with his own otherness. This moment of "auto-destruction" begins with an expression of hatred towards one's neighbor. Fanon analyzes this "irrationality" as the direct consequence of the material conditions of colonial rule. Also pertinent here is the other great anticolonial figure Mohandas Gandhi who, for all that his name is synonymous with nonviolent struggle, was nevertheless wholly invested in the death drive. Satyagraha or soul force is the practice of turning the affect of anticolonial aggression upon oneself—starve oneself, lay oneself deliberately open to the violence of the state to court death.

Political struggle and the death drive are imbricated because intersubjectivity begins with the subject him/herself. Are we not all other first and selves later, others to ourselves? I am concerned that if we do not acknowledge this, we will certainly fall into the abstract and de-historicized binary that you rightly despise—the autonomous self versus the externalized other object. So, while I agree with you about the perniciousness of the foundational fantasy of individual autonomy, I am unsure about the function of negative affects and drives, those quintessential human potentialities, as constitutive of that autonomy. My question is, can we think of intersubjectivity, political and interpersonal as occurring through rather than despite the process of negative transmission of affect? Can negative affects sometimes have positive effects?

This brings me to the other issue in this manuscript that I find enigmatic, but full of possibilities. I will focus on two points you make about language and its relation to affect. First, you propose that the transmission of affect need not be necessarily mediated by language. "You dump when your voice tones are violently angry, and another's sense of well-being is shaken by those invisible violent vibrations" (Brennan MS, 53). It is not what one is actually saying, but the tone of voice that causes the ripples rocking the other's equilibrium. Here, the affect rides on the back of language, but it is not subsumed by it. Rather, the affect is thrown by language, and in its separation it is nevertheless a form of knowledge and a profound experience of the other. The transmission itself then is wordless; but as I understand it, it can be known only in its disengagement from language.

I am reminded here of Agamben's concept of infancy, as a mute experience that is not merely a deficiency of words, but a human potentiality that exists in the break between langue and parole, language and speech. For Agamben, the subject is a subject only in language and infancy, or the kind of intersubjectivity that I understand you to be delineating is not prior to language, but "coexists in its origins with language" (Agamben 1993, 48). We cannot "reach infancy" he writes, "without encountering language" (48.). What your work underlines, within this problematic as defined by Agamben, is the proposition that this wordless experience is essentially a transmission. It is not merely a human potentiality, but it is an intersubjective one. I find this inordinately useful in breaking down the anthropocentrism of Agamben's analysis which enables me to pursue the question of language in its relation to wordlessness and the voice as the vanishing point of the human.

Second, in the last chapter, you propose that the fleshly codes, such as DNA, the drives, erotic energy and biological rhythms, are structured like languages and are "intelligent systems of communication" like linguistic communication. I find this to be an alluvial concept, rich with deposits for furthering feminist inquiry and perhaps our thinking about sexuality and politics. Your view that we can attribute the denigration of biological codes as less intelligent than linguistic communication to the over-valorization of the subject is very persuasive. You write:

> The linguistic chain is split from the other chains of meaning and logic—hormones—genetic codes—solar systems—by the insertion of the subject-position where it does not belong. That is to say, I am arguing that without this insertion, the structure of the linguistic chain is homologous with that of other living chains, living sequences whose interaction determines the extent of the life drive. (Brennan MS, 253b)

My sense is that Lacan, whom you relegate to your opposite camp, can be read in support of this point. His theory of the end of analysis and the need to bring drive and desire into syncopation with each other, his elaboration of bodily organs, theory of the lamella, of mortality and immortality, etc. are all oriented ethically towards the revelation of the subject's decentered position with regard to the Other.

What I am uncertain about is the consequence that you draw from the realignment of the various bodily and linguistic codes. You suggest that by eliminating the subject as the center of knowledge, adopting a more heliocentric view, will extend our "imaginary visualization" (ibid., 260b) and permit us to reject a common sense perspective founded on empirical observation and to behold the systematicity of logic and reason. But it is not at all clear to me how such rationalism dispenses with the subject. I worry that the abstraction of logic and reason from sensory perception paradoxically dematerializes the body rather than materializing reason.

The last point I want to make concerns your thesis that the transmission of affect has today become largely unconscious and has faded from everyday cultural consciousness altogether as a form of knowledge. I do not dispute your claim that intersubjectivity or wordless communication, if asserted as ontological givens, would be viewed with horror because it threatens contemporary fantasies of autonomy. However, my sense is that today the transmission of affect has not so much been relegated to the unconscious as it is thoroughly instrumentalized by technology and capitalism. Is not western society thoroughly overcome by the continual and ever rapid transmission of affects to the point that singularity and agency, even as they are fantasized as inalienable properties of citizenship, have been thoroughly eroded?

Consider for a moment the function of technology in our societies—its control, proliferation and instrumentalization of rhetorics. Televised wars and disasters, internet porn, internet relationships, reality cameras, wall street and the stock market, shopping to cure depression and loneliness, phrases like consumer confidence, that directly translate into GDP, and Joseph Pines and James Gilmore's book *Experience Economy,* where "work is theater and every business a stage" etc. Are these anything but forms of knowledge, or more properly modes of information, that convert the transmission of affect into capital? Atmosphere, mood, feelings, states of mind such as well-being, depression, disorder, harmony, have all been converted into information flows, stimulated and orchestrated by a team of experts that includes doctors, psychologists, spiritual healers, design experts, marketing teams, product managers, and consumers. Affect is the paper that value is printed on, so we cannot really speak in any certain terms about health and "furtherance of the body's good" as the essence of rationality and reality (Brennan MS, 265b).

In commodity culture, the good is mediated by capital as goods, and is the transmission of surplus value generated by the alienation of labor and the fetishization of commodities. The life drive then functions in the service of reproduction, not of life but of live trade, producing more labor in the service of the transmission of affect/capital. This materialist view obviously does not contradict your thesis at all. I am sure that you will agree that there is a concrete economic dimension to the transmission of affects as blockages to our feelings, and that it is the quantified management of affects by the experience economy that we must oppose. What shifts with the introduction of this perspective is our understanding of how the good can be defined and accessed.

To conclude, I come back to the death drive as the possible interruption of the violent cycle of instrumentalized affect. We confront an abyss where neither words nor affects or emotions, have any transmissibility. But the death drive, as Lacan reminds us, is to be distinguished from the death instinct. The latter is entropic and aims at a state of inertia, whereas the death drive is about a radical halting, about surprise—the possibility of the emergence of the completely and radically new, as a time when even expectation and anticipation are held in suspension.

Teresa, you have taught us this by your own life example: Dying, in a sense, is the great discerning moment of the body. The body in an ontic sense may pass, but to believe that this is a point of closure is to give in to inertia. After all, the "thoughtful living body," riddled by the drives, is immortal.

Notes

1. In writing this essay, I have used the manuscript that Teresa sent me in 2002, well before the book appeared in print. The quotations and pagination, therefore, refer to the manuscript version and not to the book. My in text citations of the manuscript version appear as "(Brennan MS, page no.)." The pagination on the manuscript is however inconsistent and proceeds as follows: Chapters 1 through 4 are numbered sequentially and end on page 144; Chapter 5, pages 203–232; Chapter 6, pages 245–281; Chapter 7, 245–276 (b). Since Chapter 7 has the same pagination as Chapter 6, I have named the second set of 245 and following pages "b."

2. Jacques Alain Miller, connects the concept of the body, our imaginary dis-identification with it, and the drives. He speaks of the theory of the body in Lacanian psychoanalysis where a distinction is made between the terms "life" and the "body." The body as One, as a unity, is of the imaginary order, whereas life, or the living body, is perhaps of the order of the Real, conceivable as a colony of multi-organisms and molecules; it is translatable into a kind of hylozoism, a notion dependent on matter as monistic. Such a view of the living body has the consequence of negating the distinction between life and death. Miller paraphrases Diderot: "Living, I act and react in mass. Dead, I act and react in molecules" (Miller 2001, 11). There is an inherent connection then between the experience of the living body—the body in pieces—and the drive. For drives, as we may recall from Lacan's Seminar XI, emerge from part objects—the rims of the body. The drives are primarily a memorial to the lost organ of the libido, which Lacan terms as the mythical lamella, the thing of immortality. The drives incarnate the loss of immortality by giving body to the various *objets petit a* (partial representatives of the immortal lamella) such as gaze, voice, breast, phallus, feces. Not only do all drives, themselves partial, arise from part objects, rims or orifices of the body, but also as Miller puts it "[Lacan] represents for us the libido as an organ, as an object, but an object endowed with a deadly sense. He defines the libido under the form of the myth, as a being carrier of death" (ibid., 28). All drives are death drives in the sense that they memorialize our lost immortality once materialized by the mythical organ of the libido, the lamella. What is significant about this notion of the death drive is that it locates itself at the seam where the Freudian opposition between the sexual drive and the death drive intersect with each other and become one.

References

Agamben, Giorgio. 1993. *Infancy and History: Essays on the Destruction of Experience*. Trans. Liz Heron. New York: Verso.

Brennan, Teresa. 2004. *The Transmission of Affect*. Ithaca: Cornell University Press.

———1993. *History After Lacan*. London: Routledge.

Fanon, Frantz. 1963. *The Wretched of the Earth*. Trans. Constance Farrington. New York: Grove Press.

Freud, Sigmund. 1963. "The Unconscious." In *General Psychological Theory*, Philip Rieff, ed., Cecil M. Baines, trans. New York: Collier Books, 116–150. Originally published in 1915.

————1961. *Beyond the Pleasure Principle*. Trans. James Strachey. New York: Norton.

————1949. *An Outline of Psycho-Analysis*. Trans. James Strachey. New York: Norton.

Herrnstein, Richard and Charles Murray. 1994. *The Bell Curve: Intelligence and Class Structure in American Life*. New York: Simon and Schuster.

Lacan, Jacques. 1992. *The Ethics of Psychoanalysis: The Seminar of Jacques Lacan VII, 1959–1960*. Trans. Dennis Porter. New York: Norton.

Miller, Jacques Alain. 2001. "Lacanian Biology and the Event of the Body." Trans. Barbara P. Fulks and Jorge Jauregui. *Lacanian Ink* 18 (Spring): 6–29.

Pine, Joseph and James Gilmore. 1999. *The Experience Economy*. Cambridge: Harvard Business School.

CHAPTER EIGHT

Ubuntu and Teresa Brennan's Energetics

———— ⚬〰⚬ ————

Drucilla Cornell

TERESA BRENNAN WAS A visionary thinker. At the heart of her vision was a passionate plea for all of us to take up the battle for what she called an "economy of generosity," and if not that, at least an "economy of sustenance." These two economies would be pitted against the fantasized, or what Brennan calls "the fundamental hallucination" upon which advanced capitalism rests—a fantasized economy of scarcity. The scarcity is a fantasy because, first, it belies the possibility of different forms of redistribution of resources as impossible. Secondly, and based on the first aspect of the fantasy, the purported scarcity, it also rejects completely the idea that if human creativity were allowed to operate with full force against the fixity of capitalist relations of production, we could find our way back to a "saving" energetic exchange with nature. This "generous" or "saving" economy would not only provide human beings throughout the world with sustenance, but would also allow us to explore new ways of living together in our planet, based on an energetic exchange with nature and ourselves that would allow us to be constantly in motion in how we shape the world together.

Although this vision may at first glance seem utopian, most of Brennan's work was directed to showing us how it need not be so conceived. Her originality was to connect Freudian psychoanalysis with what she saw as the foundational hallucination of constructed inertia. This foundational hallucination was inseparable for Brennan from how the modern ego is constructed as a purportedly discrete entity. That entity seeks to contain its own "energetic overflows," and by endlessly struggling to maintain itself against others seeks to control any disturbance in the fantasized equilibrium that protects its discreteness. In other words, the pathways of energy become blocked. It is this subject centered blockage that, for Brennan, marks the modern ego. Indeed, Brennan explains and brings our attention to this problem, including the problem Freud named but could not explain: the death drive. For Brennan,

unconscious only to limit the full reach of the insight.
llucination denies the mother-other and its absolute
entive energy of that other not only as soon as life
utero, but also as it energizes itself as it grows within
. To quote Brennan:

while the subject's fixity does in fact make it distinct relative to a state
of more rapid and interconnected motion, fixity can only make the subject
distinct, after birth, if the state of more rapid motion is not confined to the
womb. This means there has to be a field of contrast which has the same
effects and the same benefits as the flesh, but which is lived in after birth.
The obvious candidate for this field of contrast is the unbound primary process, the life drive, but what is that, other than nature? To nature overall I
have attributed the same process of connection and inherent logic, the same
inseparability of thought and substance experienced *in utero*. This attribution will make more sense if we note that the split between mind and matter, as it has been described here, is also the split between the individual and
the environment. This has to be so by the implications of this argument so
far. We can only be self-contained in relation to an environment with which
we are potentially connected. The boundary the subject erects is a boundary
against freely mobile energy and excitations in general. The contrast with
the intrauterine state explains the omnipotent aim of the pathways that
redirect the life drive on the basis of fixed points, but the experience of the
intrauterine contrast is not the end of the experience of more rapid motion.
(Brennan 2000, 68)

To release ourselves from this foundational hallucination demands the
primary recognition that the boundaries that construct the so-called limits of
the ego can never be preset. It would be no exaggeration to argue that Brennan's entire work was geared towards showing us that if a generous economy
can come into being, we must first understand what prevents it from existing. Her persistent argument that she was not utopian came from a lifelong
reworking of the idea that there is a fundamental connection between Freud's
own self-contained energetic model of the psyche and a more foundational
fantasy of the construction of the economics of scarcity that in turn bolsters
the ideologies of capitalism.

Brennan is not alone in writing about an economics of generosity that
might be beyond the self-contained model of the ego. Elizabeth Grosz in her
brilliant writing on Deleuze, and her own work on time and space,[1] has also
emphasized that the "physics" of how we negotiate our relations in space
and time with one another is crucial both to how bodies come to matter[2]
in their sexual difference, and to how the feminine in particular comes to
be identified with this generous economy. Grosz also points out that the

rethinking of physics as a different social energetics is also crucial to the writing of Luce Irigaray.

Although Brennan herself never wanted to identify those forms of motion and energy that surpass boundaries of the ego in a life-enhancing way with feminine sexuality, she also sought with these other thinkers, to try to show us how this identification comes to take place, and why feminism has at its heart the undoing of the boundaries that mark femininity as the other to the ego. For Brennan, this meant that we must come to understand how psychical reality is actually formed at a crucial moment of repression in which psychoanalysts, including the most original for Brennan, Freud and Lacan, construct a mirror stage in which it is only the mother's passive mirroring that counts, and not her actual active attention. Imagining the feminine as a passive mirror for Brennan is crucial for this foundational fantasy where the ego is an already consolidated whole that is simply mirrored by the mother rather than shaped by her. To quote Brennan again:

> From this standpoint, and given the idea that 'phantasy is the first invader,' there is, after all, something in the seduction theory that gave birth to Freud's mistakes about femininity. There is even more to it if one accepts that psychical reality is constituted by a repressed fixed point and the secondary inertia, the feminine fixity which overlays it. In fixing the feminine, the father, like the man, may make his daughter the second still point, the second border that makes femininity literally borderline. However, contra the seduction theory, whether the father gives rather than receives is an open question, and this idea that he gives is reinforced by this: the girl, like the boy, functions ego-syntonically until puberty. Usually it is only after her own drives are reactivated, and interlock with the projections of masculine others, that involution comes into being. (Brennan 1992, 234)

Brennan's argument is that femininity in both men and women is a drain of energy. In women, those who take on femininity as a sexual identity, this drain keeps them from being effective in the world in the sense of even the most basic ego tasks that Freud himself marked out, such as directing attention and activity towards reality, and maintaining itself over time as the site of its accomplishments. Women's egos are "weak" because of the lack of directive attention that supports them from either actual fathers or symbolic fathers who, at least in patriarchal society, are identified with the phallic power to confer on the next generation a continuing sense of ego-strength. For Brennan, the facilitating phallic identity, is masculine only by convention. And yet, it is this convention that shapes masculine narcissism and feminine masochism as different orientations towards the need to struggle with all forms of energetic interplay, including aggression. For Brennan, the crucial problem of femininity is that it is dependent upon the imprint of the father and active

support of the daughter's desire. The father then, either symbolic or biological, must recognize and permit her own fantasies. The feminine mother-other
on the other hand is imagined as impotent and in her passivity incapable of
facilitating in the daughter a positive ego identity.

Following well received interpretations of psychoanalytic theory, Brennan shows us how the identification of the father with activity places him in
the position to be seen by the child as the one whose engagement bestows an
identity that like him, promotes effective agency in the world. The idea here
is simple. Since the father is identified with both activity and authority, it is
his authority that both boys and girls will look to for confirmation that they
can be egos like him. Therefore, it is his active involvement with the daughter's life that is crucial for the daughter's basic sense of life. The denial of
the economy of attention for Brennan, including in its full force as a primary
repression, leads men to be dependent on others' admiration, particularly the
admiration of women so as to constantly prop up the all-too-fragile ego, once
the father's attention has become both facilitating and potentially castrat-
ing. To summarize Brennan's ultimate point, the ego only acquires coherence
through the active attention and energetic involvement with another; and
that if we remember this physical force, it could potentially countermand the
trend towards inertia, which marks the construction of the ego, and tends
to make the ego over-active because it seeks what it cannot give itself. In
Lacanian terms, the imaginary unity of the mirror-stage denies this energetic
exchange. To quote Brennan herself, " . . . the ultimate lesson is that the
unthematized question of the permeability . . . depends on the neglect of the
physical connections between beings, connections that enable the imprints
of the one to affect the other" (Brennan 1992, 236).

My goal here is not to defend Brennan's own formulation of the significance of this idea of our psychic permeability for the construction of masculinity and femininity. Clearly there are also huge questions that remain about
the relationship between the economy of inertia that Brennan argues is integral to ego construction and the economy of scarcity that Brennan defines as
governing advanced capitalist ideology. Brennan's latest books are suggestive
and provocative in how we might think about those connections. The question that she continuously hammers on us to ask is: What is the relationship
between any of the formulations of the individual as a bounded entity, formulations that have obviously dominated Western philosophy in the modern
age, and political and ethical arguments that we can never overcome capitalism because it is the way of life and the mode of production best formulated
for maintaining the freedom of these discrete entities we call individuals?

Brennan was daring, although, not alone amongst important feminist
thinkers, in demanding that we think about the permeability of our proposed
ego-boundaries in an energetic field shaped by others. Her argument about

energy was often controversial because it runs up against some of our (and by 'our' I mean Western or European) conceptions of individuality, because they have turned on the postulate that we are discrete individuals. Western political philosophy has generally taken it from there. Think, for example, of social contract theories, which despite all the crucial differences between them, always postulate an individual that contracts with other individuals. The boundedness of these individuals is assumed; the only imagined connection that can be fair to those individuals is in turn envisioned as a contract.

Yet, once we leave the boundaries of Europe, this one particular notion of individuality clearly does not rule. In the last year, I've been involved in a project to study the meaning of *ubuntu* in South Africa. *Ubuntu* was a word that appeared in the 1993 preamble of the South African Constitution, and has been used in constitutional and other legal decisions in South Africa. *Ubuntu* has been difficult for Europeans to understand; my fieldwork helps us explain why.[3]

Ubuntu, crudely translated, means "humanity," but this is not humanity understood philosophically as human nature, or even humanity conceived as an ideal. Humanity is constantly shaped and reshaped, as I learned slowly in my interviews, as we interact with one another in an ethical relationship that we can never escape. We are always forming and reforming ourselves together and through one another. Even the language of "drain" is not adequate here, because what one gives in support of the community would not be grasped as a drain on the self. We can begin to see how Brennan's own language, particularly when she writes that women give too much of their energy away to others, can itself be seen to be still ensnared in the idea of the ego that she sought so hard to criticize.

In one of my interviews, a woman tried to explain why *ubuntu* is not altruism. As she put it, "what goes out through the front door comes in through the back window. You may not know when, you may not know how, but you can know that it will always come in through the back window." Another famous expression of *ubuntu* also described by this woman, is that a person with *ubuntu* is the one "whose path is well beaten, because everyone knows that she will always be there for them."[4]

Ubuntu then is not altruism because altruism separates the idea of self-interest from the idea of helping others. But if we are all bounded together in the shape we give to our humanity, and the humanity that we ourselves come to represent to others, then it makes no sense to make this kind of separation. *Ubuntu* in this sense is an interactive ethic in which we are constantly bringing our humanity into a new form. There can be no preset boundaries because who and how we can be together is always something that we are shaping as we interact with one another with the full knowledge that we are always interdependent.

Ubuntu is integrally connected to another concept called *seriti*, which names the life force or force field that both shapes individuals and communities. We can understand this idea of *seriti* through the image of magnetization. Each person is a magnet, creating together a complex field. Any change in the degree of magnetization of one will affect the magnetization of all. But in a like manner, it is the magnetic field itself that in a sense creates magnetic force, including the magnetic force of the individual. This interactive nature of both *seriti* and *ubuntu* is crucial to the different way of thinking about individuality.

Against stereotypes of African communalism, individuality and free will are often spoken about as being what respect for *ubuntu* ultimately achieves. To quote another interview, "I never would be who I am and the way I am if I did not have all those in the past loving me and affirming me. I am as good as they helped make me be, and let me be." Again, to quote this same interview, "I am a law student now, and without the support of my entire family, I never would have dreamed of becoming a lawyer." Individuality then is seen as something that is given to us not only in our present communities, but intergenerationally.

The closest analogue to *ubuntu* in the Western philosophical canon is through the philosopher Hegel and his concept of objective community, or *sittlichkeit*, that always precedes and constitutes the subject of rights. Hegel famously defined exactly what the boundaries were between all those aspects of the community and indeed of the nation-state, as if the final form of all of humanity had been given, at least on the level of the ideal. *Ubuntu* runs in exactly the opposite direction; and it is precisely in Brennan's sense that it moves counter to set boundaries by keeping the energetic interplay between people and interaction as the only limit on what might be possible.

Ubuntu has sometimes been used conservatively, as when it appeals to subsidiarity, by which people are placed in a hierarchy of benevolent paternalism, including women under some customary law systems in South Africa. But even if certain aspects of customary law became rigidified through an appeal to subsidiarity, *ubuntu* as a dynamic social ethic can always be relied upon to make fluid again what had come to be consolidated as necessary to custom. Subsidiarity denotes that each one of us has a proper place in society and our obligations flow from status and kinship connections.

The potential for a conservative reading of subsidiarity is that it freezes hierarchies of gender. Subsidiarity need not be read that way since it also includes the idea that each one of us takes up such changing obligations along the ebbs and flows of time throughout an individual human life. An adult, for example, has different obligations than a child; an older person has the right of respect from everyone younger than her; and even in the most sexist readings of subsidiarity both husbands and wives, and men and women more generally, have obligations to one another. Again, to quote one of my interviews, "when I demand *ubuntu*, I demand that I be seen as someone who shapes his community as much as any man."

Some western intellectual circles that presume an individual imagined to exist outside of society have difficulty in understanding *ubuntu* precisely because it implies a force field through which individuals both shape and are shaped in turn. In other words, *Ubuntu* explicitly rejects the notion of a pre-given person. Personhood is always a gift to us by those who sustain us, and recognize and facilitate our coming into our singularity.

Why does there seem to be an inevitable ethical dimension to *ubuntu*? It is precisely because "*ubuntu* thinking" recognizes the lesson that Brennan has tried so hard to teach us. That the remembrance of our interdependence, our fundamental acknowledgement of how we are the person we seek to be, is only because we are gathered together as a person by others, and sustained by them in that self-gathering. In remembering our interdependence, including our intergenerational connections with others, not just with the living but also with the dead, we are called to responsibility to that community. This is completely irreducible to our European vision of the social contract. Obligation and duty in this sense go way beyond that which is allowable under social contract theory. Because we are a magnetic force ourselves, the power we have to shape our community is thought to reinforce that responsibility.

I do not pretend to be giving the reader the last word on *ubuntu*; or perhaps more profoundly, there could be no last word on *ubuntu*, understood as a humanity that is always reshaping itself and the force field in which it comes to be. We have to be brave enough to ask the question, would the Truth and Reconciliation Commission[5] even have been possible without something like this other understanding of our interdependence?

Evidently the concept of *seriti* as a force field that shapes who we can be can also diminish us if we cannot live up to its demand for responsibility. *Ubuntu* and the corresponding cluster of concepts that I have described are informed by a very different notion of the person than even the one offered by Brennan; she remained committed to a bounded ego in a way that is foreign to ubuntu even as it supports and proclaims the importance of freedom for each one of us.

The difference here might be that Brennan seems to indicate that interdependence itself might be a drain; although, of course, in her more visionary works she tries to point to a more thoughtful interdependence that would not result in such a drain. Brennan is at times conflicted on this matter, and sometimes her examples such as the father/daughter energy exchange becomes generalized to the point that this interdependence, in the peculiar feminine sense of pleasing that comes in the form of reactive obligation, can only be overcome through increased boundaries for the ego. This is perhaps not so much a weakness in Brennan but an indicator of how difficult it is for any of us to imagine energizing, interdependent relationships in which we gladly take up our obligations because of an acceptance of being a part of a community that gives to us so as to allow us to "come into our own"—a phrase I am using more loosely here than in the traditional psychoanalytic sense.

Thus if we live in a society dominated by vengeance, then all of us will be shaped by that vengeance, not simply those who are actually involved in the acts of revenge. This is why in South Africa the death penalty is disallowed, because it would shape a society based on the legal authorization of vengeance, and this legal authorization would then be shaped by the vengeance that it had unleashed.

Ubuntu can perhaps help many of us to understand the sense that I certainly have that my life and the world in which I live has been altered by the death of Teresa Brennan. Mourning for one person is not simply an individual psychic activity in which I slowly learn to come to terms with the lost object by internalizing her and what was best in my relationship to her. That understanding of mourning itself turns on a conception of psychic life as a bounded discrete entity that we think of as the individual ego, even with the addition of the unconscious. If we are truly shaped in a force field and we are bounded together, then the passing of one of us changes the shape of the field.

What then does it mean for us to mourn Teresa Brennan? It means for us to remember her wisest lesson—a lesson that I heard and have learned so much from in my work in South Africa. When one of us is fatally injured, particularly as Teresa was, alone on that road in Florida, something happens that indicates the shape of our own community of feminist scholars. Her absence demands that we try to face how we have shaped ourselves and how we might reform ourselves to acknowledge both the significance of her life, and the significance of our loss.

Notes

1. See Elizabeth Grosz, *Space Time and Perversion* (New York: Routledge, 1995) and *Volatile Bodies* (Bloomington: Indiana University Press, 1994).

2. Judith Butler, *Bodies That Matter* (New York: Routledge, 1993).

3. Drucilla Cornell, "A Preliminary Summation of the *Ubuntu* Project" and "The Relevance of Political Theory to the *Ubuntu* Project," (unpublished manuscripts on file with the author).

4. Interviews on file with the author.

5. The Truth and Reconciliation Commission was constructed by the new government led by Nelson Mandella as an institutional forum in which both victims and perpetrators would confront each other in public. Although the Truth and Reconciliation Commission had a legal aspect in that some victims of apartheid were appealing for some retribution and reparation and some perpetrators were demanding amnesty, these legal duties did not encompass its primary and more symbolic task which was to create a space in which the horrifying suffering of apartheid could be heard.

References

Brennan, Teresa. 2000. *Exhausting Modernity: Grounds for a New Economy*. London: Routledge.

————1992. *The Interpretation of the Flesh: Freud and Femininity*. London: Routledge.

CHAPTER NINE

What's Not Seen

‒‒‒‒‒‒‒⟨◌◌⟩‒‒‒‒‒‒‒

Gillian Beer

TERESA RESPONDED WITH ALL her senses, intellectually. She explored knowledge and knowledges with a mix of lightness and intensity. She understood that we cannot know enough to satisfy the cravings of epistemophilia (the thirst for knowledge that some analysts identify with the infant's first thirst). She was clear-sighted about the identification of seeing with intellectual life, about its insufficiency and yet its necessary fund of metaphors with which to work our imaginations, as in "being clearsighted." She relished the material in all its sensory manifestations—margarita cocktails, clothes, music, sea-bathing, and the body in all its satisfactions, above all, in its capacity for conversation, in which mind and voice, breath and ambient atmosphere, tension and attraction, combine.

Her move askance from the mind-body problem shrugged off fixed polarities and allowed her to ask new questions, such as the one that opens her most recent book, *The Transmission of Affect* (2004). We enter a room, there is an "atmosphere"; how can we analyze what we so well recognize? Should we set aside questions for which philosophy seems not to provide tools for an answer? Her answer is that we should address such questions with every kind of evidence we can command—or perhaps a better word, evoke. Teresa worked with fugitive experience, as well as with what endures; she responded to the intricacy of the instant as well as to that which has been severely argued over time.

One of my most memorable conversations with her concerned, not the gaze but the glance, the unavoidable revelation of other peoples' business that the eye seizes before it has a chance to censor itself. We talked about the pleasures of the glance—conspiratorial, provocative sometimes, often innocent of intent—seeing without prevision. We were conscious, in our talk that most things in the world are *not there* in front of our eyes at any time.

Vision includes inner images as well as what we can see at the particular moment. Memory provides a constant kaleidoscope of images with which we

101

supplement or even contradict what we see materially. Literature, I proposed, is another independent source of such images, as we read we see inside our minds, spontaneously, what is *not* before us in actuality. We see it moreover with extraordinary intensity, as the poet William Blake put it:

> To see the world in a grain of sand
> And a Heaven in a wild flower
> Hold infinity in the palm of your hand
> And eternity in an hour.[1]

Literature condenses what we see at present with what we have seen, allowing us to form intense mental and emotional images of what we may never in limited actuality see.

Teresa was acutely conscious of what we see around us in the world and of the diverse contexts for vision, not in themselves visible. The collection she introduced and edited with Martin Jay *Vision in Context* (1995),[2] explores these issues, and adumbrates what increasingly became the central topic of her work: How to escape the mind-body split; how to sustain the particular knowledge created in the gendered body as well as in its ungendered sensory resources.

In *The Space of Literature* (1955)[3] Maurice Blanchot suggests the tricky borderline that vision occupies in experience:

> Seeing presupposes distance, decisiveness which separates, the power to stay out of contact and in contact avoid confusion. Seeing means that this separation has nevertheless become an encounter. But what happens when what you see, although at a distance, seems to touch you with a gripping contact, when the manner of seeing is a kind of touch, when seeing is *contact* at a distance?

That drawing close across sensory and personal boundaries, that feeling for the haptic (touch, and seeing as touch), speaks to the work that Brennan was later to do.

Flesh and bone generate more than the five senses we can name. Changes in the social medium in which we live also shift, Teresa argues, the hormonal disposition of the body, and thus its capacity for affect. This two-way interaction knits the biological and the social inextricably, and shiftingly, together. This is not a neo-Lamarkian position. It does not propose either necessary improvement or decline as the outcome of accumulated memory traces. It does propose an answer to those shifts, so evident and so hard to specify, in what may loosely be called "the temper of the times." Her position demands history, and the evidence of shared as well as individual experience. It may even go as far as to offer suggestions about why ideas that are incorrigibly difficult to one generation,—taught freely in schools—fifty years later, the theory of relativity, for example, become manifest.

Recently, there has been a surge of work on affect, among neuroscientists in particular. Antonio Damasio in *The Feeling of What Happens* (1999)[4] and more recently in *Looking for Spinoza: Joy, Sorrow and the Feeling Brain* (2003) pursues a train of investigation that chimes with what Teresa sought. This fresh impulse in other fields makes it clear that her work is part of a compelling debate, and tradition of thought, reaching back to the seventeenth century. This Spinozean tradition of enquiry is newly active again, partly as an outcome of her provocations, even where these were not directly part of the disciplinary dialogue of another field. Writing about vision and what's seen, Damasio says that progress in the past twenty years has revealed "in great detail how the brain processes various aspects of vision, not just shape but color and movement too." He continues:

> Progress is also being made in the understanding of audition, touch, and smell, and at long last there is a renewed interest in the understanding of the internal senses—pain, temperature, and the like. It is fair to say, however, that we have barely begun to unravel the fine details of these systems. (Damasio 2003, 203)

Damasio's interest, properly, is in fine detail and the understanding of brain process. Teresa's is in the interaction between persons in a historical moment as well as in the interaction of the senses in solitary experience. But they share a crucial perception: "The mind [writes Damasio] exists for the body, is engaged in telling the story of the body's multifarious events, and uses that story to optimise the life of the organism" (ibid, 206). That is, the mind is of the body, not opposed to it, and is its storyteller.

In "Two Forms of Consciousness" Teresa Brennan writes:

> How then are we to reconcile this situation, where we are unconscious of that which keeps us conscious? Rather than dismiss this as a typical Freudian confusion, I want to propose that we take it literally. The issue is precisely how we stay unconscious of that which seems to be equivalent to consciousness. This means that we can recast the players here. They are not the ego and the unconscious. At least, the ego is still a player, but it is an ego that keeps itself unconscious of a certain form of consciousness. But as the ego is identified with consciousness, as it is one's conscious identity, this recasting leads in turn to the proposition that there are in fact two consciousnesses, with a repressive apparatus between them. In other words, from this standpoint, the relation between consciousness and the unconscious is actually the relation between two different forms of consciousness. (Brennan 1997, 91)

According to both Damasio and Brennan, the story being told is one that the consciousness need not—or, in Teresa's proposal, cannot—listen to. Yet this story is that which informs and sustains consciousness. It is composed by and resonates with the materials of the senses and the activities of the brain. It is realized in the full action of being and it embraces change. For Teresa, that problem of how to explain change "either in new movements or fresh ideas" is a crucial one. For an explanation to be reached she perceives that it is necessary to escape from the totalitarianism of the totally socially constructed, just as much as it is necessary to expand the reach of neuro-scientific description.

Teresa explored these insights and these dilemmas in a poem she included in a recent essay entitled, "My Open Agenda, or How Not to Make the Right Career Moves." It is the poem with which she began writing again after a period of severe trauma and when she was preoccupied with writing against the mind-body split: I quote it in full as she sent it to me. As one reads this poem it is important to respect line endings and to observe nonce spellings. These pauses and oscillations within words allow her to express in the movement of the poem the story that she seeks, a story that at the start of the poem appears voided, and absent. "Re-tyre," for example, is spelled as for re-treading a car tire rather than as withdrawal.

Plotless
Stripped of membered time
No clear cut crystal goal in view
No compass kept
No bank
No trust

My history spent
To be
Exhausted of the memories
That—in addition—numbered me

Where in the flesh of clarity
Or in the wet of unmown grass
That wraps new limbered feet

Am I

Taken by an earth
That's tired
But willing
To retyre my tread,
To reinvent, invert the line
That marks the living from the dead (Brennan 2003)

The poem expresses at once exhaustion of consciousness and the reemergence of wholeness: that reinvention, that "inversion of the line" between the living and the dead allows a passage way between states of being. Though at the time she did not foresee it, perhaps, the line of writing holds experience steady past death and allows it to find expression in an assurance that the mind-body split cannot account for. Writing, the outcome of being, sustains presence and accommodates change. It draws up into itself the materials of the senses, the activities of the brain, and marks them forward into the future. It is, in a troubled and imperfect yet compelling way, a rebuttal of the mind-body split. Bishop Drogo put it well in the eleventh century in the preamble to a charter he issued:

> Since the days of man's life do not endure for ever, our ancestors invented letters and signs . . . So, by an ingenious means, the dead might engage in conversation with the living, and might reveal the secrets of their wishes, actions and plans, to those who were to follow, even though they were manifestly separated by great distances of time and space. (Beer 1989, vi)

Knowledge is held in the *written body* of the individual; it is then continued across time and space in other beings, past "membered time." It is in that sense "what's not seen," though one compelling medium of its transmission may be inscribed signs on paper. The mind, as Spinoza defined it, is "the idea of the human body." This first perception has been developed in the work, diversely, of Damasio and Brennan, to escape the oppositional split and instead to understand the degree to which affect and knowledge compose a complex whole.

I end with a passage from John Donne, from a sermon he gave in the open air on April 22, 1622, at St Mary's, Spitalfield. It is a sermon about knowledge, about how we know on earth and shall know in heaven. I think it would provoke in Teresa that familiar gasp of pleasure, surprise, and resistance. In Heaven, says Donne:

> There we shall be as the Angels . . . our curiosity shall have this noble satisfaction, we shall know how the Angels know, by knowing as they know. We shall not pass from author to author, as in a grammar school, nor from art to art, as in a university but, as that general which knighted his whole army, God shall create us all doctors in a minute. That great library, those infinite volumes of the books of creatures shall be taken away, quite away, no more Nature; . . . the Scriptures themselves, shall be taken away; no more preaching, no more reading the Scriptures, and that great school-mistress, Experience, and Observation shall be removed, no new thing to be done, and in an instant, I shall know more than they all could reveal unto me. (Donne 1929, 737)

For Teresa the processes of knowledge finding and knowledge making engrossed a lifetime on earth and included the experience of conversion as well as of scepticism. That experience of conversion she described as "loving

intelligence" felt in the senses as well as the mind. I think she would enter the
joy of Donne's imagining of a new epistemology. His description moves from
books to nature and leaves in place until the last experience and observation.
Finally when all those resources are abandoned he imagines knowledge in
heaven experienced at once in instantaneity and eternity: the strains of epistemophilia satisfied, knowing *how* and knowing *as* combined.

Notes

1. William Blake, "Auguries of Innocence" in *William Blake: Selected Poetry and Prose*, ed. David Fuller (London: Longman, 2000), 285.

2. Also, see my essay in this volume (Brennan and Jay 1995) on the secular-izing of the invisible in the nineteenth century.

3. Maurice Blanchot, *Space of Literature: A Translation of L'espace Litteraire*, trans. Ann Smock (Lincoln: University of Nebraska Press, 1992 [1955]), 32.

4. Antonio Damasio, *The Feeling of What Happens: Body and Emotion in the Making of Consciousness* (New York and London: Harcourt, 1999).

References

Beer, Gillian. 1989. *Arguing with the Past*. London: Routledge.

Brennan, Teresa. 2004. *The Transmission of Affect*. Ithaca: Cornell University Press.

———2003. "My Open Agenda, or How Not to Make the Right Career Moves," in *Singing in the Fire: Stories of Women in Philosophy*, ed. Linda Martín Alcoff, 23–40. New York: Rowman and Littlefield.

———1997. "The Two Forms of Consciousness," *Theory, Culture, and Society* 14: 91.

Brennan, Teresa and Martin Jay, eds. 1995. *Vision in Context: Historical and Contemporary Perspectives on Sight*. New York: Routledge.

Damasio, Antonio. 2003. *Looking for Spinoza: Joy, Sorrow, and the Feeling Brain*. London: Heinemann

Donne, John. 1929. *Complete Poetry and Selected Prose*. John Hayward, ed. London: The None Such Press.

CHAPTER TEN

Reading Brennan

———❧⟨☙⟩❧———

Jane Gallop

In 1992, Teresa Brennan published her first book, *The Interpretation of the Flesh*. The book opens with two epigraphs. One is from Proust: "But at least, if strength were granted me for long enough to accomplish my work, I should not fail . . . to describe men first and foremost as occupying a place, a very considerable place compared with the restricted one which is allotted them in space, a place . . . in the dimension of Time" (Brennan 1992, vi, ellipsis mine). The epigraph ends on the word "Time," capitalized; the quotation is from "A la recherche du temps perdu" ("In Search of Time Lost"). The first chapter of Brennan's book has a section entitled "Psychical Reality: Time Lost," the last phrase alluding to Proust's "temps perdu." Time is crucial for Brennan's work. But what is most striking in this epigraph is not the abstract, capitalized "Time" on which the sentence concludes, but rather the earlier passing reference to time which resonates with the other epigraph.

The other epigraph is from Freud, from a letter to Lou Andreas-Salome:

Where is my Metapsychology? In the first place, it remains unwritten. Working-over material systematically is not possible for me; the fragmentary nature of my observations and the sporadic character of my ideas will not permit it. If, however, I should live another ten years, remain capable of work during that time . . . then I promise to make further contributions to it. (Brennan 1992, vi, ellipsis Brennan's)

Brennan's first book opens with two epigraphs: Proust on Time and Freud on Metapsychology. While Brennan's work is very much on both time and metapsychology, the two epigraphs are most evocative in the gesture they share. Proust says, "If strength were granted me for long enough to accomplish my work" (Brennan 1992, vi); Freud says, "If I should live another ten years, remain capable of work during that time." (ibid.) Both men raise the question as to whether they will have strength enough, long enough, time

107

enough to complete their work and their writing. The repetition of this thought in the two otherwise dissimilar epigraphs is striking, insistent. Looking back on it now, on Teresa's choice of these two epigraphs for her first book, this insistence becomes positively eerie. "If I should live another ten years"; in 1992 Teresa Brennan opened her book with these two epigraphs, ten years later she died.

Brennan's first book opens with two men asking if they would have enough time to get what they have to say written down. Brennan's last book, *The Transmission of Affect* (2004), begins with the reassuring thought that Teresa got it down just in time. In the foreword to *Transmission*, Teresa's longtime assistant and literary executrix Woden Teachout writes:

> The night Teresa was hit, she was working on the finishing touches of chapter four of this book . . . Teresa considered this the keystone chapter, not only of *The Transmission of Affect* but also of her work as a whole. A few weeks earlier she had declared herself done with the chapter. As she pressed 'save,' she turned to me and said, 'Now I've said what I've been trying to say for twenty-five years.' (Brennan 2004, x–xi)

As comforting as I find these words, I remain nonetheless unsettled by the uncanniness of those two epigraphs Teresa chose in 1992. Whereas the executrix's foreword might lay this worry to rest, we find something else in Teresa's own introduction to her last book.

Chapter 1 of *The Transmission of Affect* is entitled "Introduction." In the first section of that introduction, Brennan explains how, in the transmission of an affect from one person to another, "the content one person gives to" the affect "may be very different from the content given to the same affect by another" (Brennan 2004, 6). She moves to an example presumably in order to be sure her reader is with her. Here she draws close to the reader by moving into first and second person pronouns:

> If I pick up on your depression, my focus perhaps will be on my unfinished book. Yours, more seriously, may be on the loss of a loved person. I may be somewhat startled, if I reflect on it, to find such depression on my part in relation to my unfinished book, which may be a bit depressing to have undone but which should not feel like death. (Brennan 2004, 6–7)

Brennan's point here is that "even if I am picking up on your affect . . . the thoughts I attach to that affect remain my own" (Brennan 2004, 6). But reading her example now, its effect far exceeds her intended point. "My unfinished book . . . should not feel like death," she tells us, but for us reading it now, her "unfinished book" feels precisely like death.

Examples are, generically, gestures toward the reader; the author is trying to assure that the reader gets the point and is not lost or left behind. This sort of example ("I," "you") is a site where the author reaches out to the reader, seems to speak directly to us. The first and second person pronouns make it sound like a conversation between two people in a room talking to one another. That fiction of a conversation, of talking rather than writing, of co-presence, underwrites this example in particular. Because Brennan is imagining she is picking up the reader's affects.

As I understand Brennan's theory, affects are transmitted physically, through the senses, chemically and rhythmically. They are, as she puts it, "literally in the air"; "in the room." To imagine affects transmitted from the reader to the author is to imagine the reader in the room. This example imagines us there with her, at some moment before the book is finished, at some moment when she is worried about the fact that the book isn't finished.

The example from the introduction to *The Transmission of Affect* imagines a scene like the one we find in the foreword to that book. In the foreword, Teachout recounts a moment when she was literally in the room as Teresa was writing. The example in the introduction imagines the reader, now the generic reader, in the place of that first privileged personal reader. Whereas Teachout was there for a moment of triumph, we are "there" at a moment when Brennan is not sure she will get it said.

While the exemplary scene of the reader transmitting affects to the author is irremediably imaginary, fictive, it turns out, from our present perspective, to also be, in some strange way, true. Brennan imagines a moment when she would be thinking about her "unfinished book" and her reader would be thinking of "the loss of a loved person."

The Transmission of Affect was published posthumously. What for her is the worry she won't finish her book becomes for the reader our loss of her.

It is uncanny to read this now; all the more so when we recall the epigraphs to her first book. Both the example from *Transmission* and the 1992 epigraphs bespeak a connection between unfinished books and death—a connection not explicitly formulated by Brennan but somehow haunting her text, hanging out in the margins, where we might not have noticed it in 1992, or if her last book wasn't posthumous.

By bringing forth this connection, I am *not* trying to say that Brennan's last book, *The Transmission of Affect* is incomplete. With all its chapters written to the end, what we have is *by no means* a fragment. When Teresa died, she was polishing not drafting.

The Transmission of Affect opens with a note, unsigned, which appears a page before Teachout's foreword. The note tells us that Teresa was "in the final stages of editing *The Transmission of Affect* in December 2002." "[O]n the night of the accident," the note goes on to say, she "had been working on the finishing touches of her favorite chapter and reviewing the copyedited version of the manuscript" (Brennan 2004, vi). That the manuscript had been copyedited implies Brennan had already declared the book complete enough to submit to the press.

"The finishing touches of her favorite chapter," "the final stages of editing," "final stages," "finishing touches"—this note insists on how very late in the process she was when she died and how very close to complete the book was. The note ends by telling us that she did not have a chance to complete the review of the copyedited manuscript, and that "the remaining review was completed by . . . Woden Teachout and . . . Sandy Hart." In other words, the note assures us that Brennan was close to done and also tells us that there was still work to do, work that had to be done by someone else when Teresa died.

This authoritative but unsigned note is immediately followed by Teachout's foreword. In the foreword, as I mentioned earlier, we can read Teresa saying, "Now I've said what I've been trying to say for twenty-five years." But immediately after that happy quote, in the very next sentence of the foreword, Teachout goes on to say: "This didn't stop her from tinkering: all her assistants knew that the only way to get her to release a book was to take it forcibly from her." Teachout's remark suggests that, left to her own devices, Teresa would not, could not, finish a book; That the stage she was in when she died—"finishing touches"—although it might have been the final stage was nonetheless a stage that threatened to go on and on, interminably. It also suggests that, for Brennan as a writer, the question of whether a book was in fact finished or not was an extremely difficult question, one she was unable to answer on her own.

The drama of the assistants "forcibly" taking the book from Teresa suggests that, in needing her assistants to reach completion, her last book while posthumous was not unique. Needing someone else to bring it to completion was the typical condition of Brennan's books. Very much in consonance with those epigraphs to her first book, the story in the front matter of her last book allows us to see that for Brennan it was always a drama, a real question, as to whether a book would be finished.

It is my uncanny sense that Teresa dying and leaving a book that was and was not finished is not only a horrid accident but is also incredibly resonant with the way she seemed to think about books and finishing. Even that something we might want theoretically to call death—and "death" is a major theoretical force in Brennan's work—is entwined with this question about finishing books.

Although I'd love to be able to say more about that, there are in fact two things I want to talk about; I need to turn now to the second. While I would like to be able to end by connecting thing one and thing two, I suspect I will have to be content with a disjointed two-part paper. So now let me turn from item #1 in my paper to item #2.

Where Thing One began at the very beginning of Brennan's first book—and tended to hang out in beginnings, in prefatory material—I found Thing Two in the last chapter of her last book.

The chapter Teresa was working on the night she was hit, the chapter Teachout calls the "keystone chapter" of Brennan's work as a whole, is not the final chapter of *The Transmission of Affect*. It is in fact, as the phrase "keystone chapter" implies, the middle chapter, fourth of seven. Chapter seven, the final chapter of her last book, is in fact entitled, "Interpreting the Flesh," a title very close to that of her first book, *The Interpretation of the Flesh*. Despite all I've said in the first half of this paper I cannot help but find this return neat, this circle satisfying and reassuring, as if she had indeed reached the end of what she had "been trying to say for twenty-five years."

As tempting as it might be to read that final chapter as a revision, putting finishing touches on her first book will not be my topic here. To do that would be to have a grand, encompassing understanding of Brennan's work. Instead, I would like to pick at one thread in Brennan's final chapter, to pull one minor thread out of the dense and complex weave of her oeuvre.

To read like that, "close reading" a small bit of a rich and energetic theoretical text, is what I do, the only way I really am able to read. But it also has the advantage that rather than making Brennan into a monument—massive, imposing, and still—it leaves us with an image of her thought very much alive and moving.

In the last chapter of *Transmission*, I was struck by a persistent value, an axiological binary that appears mainly in the adjectives. To put it simply: fast is good, slow is bad. What I want to do for the rest of this paper is consider Brennan's very insistent preference for speed.

I should confess that this preference struck me because, while I often agree with Brennan, I do not share this particular orientation. Theoretically, I tend to privilege slow over fast. To make the contrast sharper, let me say that whereas Brennan connects slowness with the ego and with thought cut off from bodily sensation, I on the other hand advocate slowing down as a way of circumventing the familiar ego paths, as a way of giving our thought access to our feelings. I share with Brennan a dislike for the sort of thought dominated by ego, for mind split from the body; we very much share the project to reconnect thought to feeling. However, whereas I associate good, connected thinking with slowing down, she characterizes good, connected thinking as fast.

In the last chapter of *Transmission*, Brennan argues for the limitations of reflective consciousness, the limitations of the ego and of thought severed from physical sensation. She tentatively proposes a model for a new "I." Not only is she proposing better psychological and epistemological models, but she is putting forth a better way of living and of thinking. To persuade us that this "other I" is better she consistently says that it is faster.

Brennan is, to be sure, explicitly uncomfortable with her terminology here, hesitant. She refers to the "other I," yet that seems wrong to her. She at times uses "soul" but that seems tentative. The distinction she uses most readily is that between "the slow 'I' and the faster 'I.'" Her longstanding interest in energy and time lead her to consistently value rapidity, consistently to castigate the ego and to chastise reflective consciousness for being slow.

To give you a general sense of the pattern, I quote four short passages from Chapter 7:

1) The ego is slower in its calculations and its ability to reach a conclusion, slower than what is commonly called intuition (Brennan 2004, 198n1).

2) [B]locks occasioned by the foundational fantasy . . . make us slower . . . by impeding the connections necessary for rapid thought and learning. The foundational fantasy removes us from the sphere of more rapid understanding, just as it slows us down in relation to the freely mobile energy into which we are born (ibid., 141).

3) Just as the subject overlays the faster world of chemical and hormonal communication . . . with the slower world contingent on seeing things from its own standpoint, so too does he lose the means for rapid interpretation of the logics of the flesh (ibid., 148).

4) [T]he body and its actions have always been ahead of the slow calculations of reflective consciousness . . . the flesh our veiled consciousness has learned to despise is faster, more intelligent, and more alive than the 'consciousness' that claims credit for its inspiration, even as it gropes around for words (ibid., 157–58).

There is much one would want to say about these passages, if I had time. To fully understand these passages would be to firmly grasp Brennan's entire theory, which would take even more time. Here I want to remark on the consistent pattern.

The ego is slow; reflective consciousness is slow; seeing things from the subject's own standpoint is slow. The foundational fantasy, which produces the subject's own standpoint, blocks and impedes us, and slows us down. Intuition is faster; chemical and hormonal communication is faster; the body and its actions, the flesh is faster. Faster is connected to more intelligent and more alive. We have been removed from the sphere of more rapid understanding; we have lost the means for rapid interpretation. We grope around for words.

Reading Brennan's last chapter, I am increasingly convinced that faster is better. I want to be freed of the blocks and impediments; I want to regain the speed I've lost.

But as someone who began reading with a prejudice in favor of slower, I am not quite ready to give in yet. Is faster always better? Is there no exception to this consistent pattern?

I find one, only one. And it is not in the final chapter; it is in the previous chapter, entitled "The Education of the Senses," a chapter devoted to Brennan's crucial notion of "discernment," which is a method for reconnecting to feeling. Discernment is the practice Brennan would have us learn—the practice that follows from her theory.

Discernment can be led astray by the ego; the ego can impede discernment in one of two ways: "discernment . . . makes mistakes when it is rushed to conclude before its time (it is rushed by the ego, which always needs a plan) or when it is delayed by the ego (which is always anxious about doing the wrong thing)" (Brennan 2004, 120). Discernment makes mistakes when it is rushed or when it is delayed. From the pattern we just looked at, we would expect the ego to "delay" discernment or slow it down. But it is equally true that the ego can impede discernment by speeding it up, by making it go faster.

Faster is not always better. There is in fact an ego-motivated speed, which Brennan calls not "faster," not "rapid," but "rushed." "Rushed to conclude before its time": makes me think of those assistants "forcibly" taking her book from her; that not only is there the fear expressed in those epigraphs of not finishing in time, there is the opposite fear of finishing prematurely, "concluding before its time."

I wish I had time to follow this through theoretically—to think about it in relation to death and writing. I would no doubt want to return to Freud's *Beyond the Pleasure Principle*—a resonant text for Brennan—and to Freud's idea that "the organism wishes to die only in its own fashion" (Freud 1955, 39) which sounds similar to not "concluding before its time."

But I don't have time to follow that theoretical path; so let me instead conclude anecdotally. While Brennan may privilege faster over slow, she nonetheless does not like "rushed." In fact, in the foreword to *The Transmission of Affect* we read that Teresa "never once rushed out the door for an airplane or an appointment. They would wait for her, she reasoned. On occasion she was wrong, but more often than not, she would emerge with a first-class seat or a particularly serendipitous social engagement as a result" (Brennan 2004, viii). Teresa never once rushed. In this glowing portrait, She has something much superior to punctuality; she has serendipity, timing. The image is one of grace and elegance: the first-class seat, others waiting for her. Her superiority is in the insistence on her own time, in the refusal to "rush."

This image of Teresa's glamorous timing—classy and elegant and magical—imbued with something we might call "discernment," is a lovely way to remember Teresa. But as a reader of Brennan's last book, I cannot help but juxtapose this lovely, gracious portrait with another image, one we find in the final chapter of *The Transmission of Affect*—an image that is the very antithesis of the woman who would not rush.

The image in the last chapter is vivid and seems gratuitous, not called for by the material. It belongs to that cruder, more primitive category of images: the simile. It is this simile that made me want to talk about the slow-fast binary. This simile seized my attention and made me feel that there was more going on behind Brennan's privileging of "faster" than it seemed. Of all the smart and important, powerful and fascinating things in Brennan's last book, this is the most unforgettable and the one that most stays with me.

The simile is an image of "groping for words," and an image that suggests how "rushing" is in fact a property not of the "faster 'I'" but of the "slow 'I.'" Here is the complete sentence: "In reality 'it' is part of something that thinks infinitely more rapidly than the secondary process that follows on behind, putting everything into words, like a middle-aged lady puffing to keep up with a train she is trying to catch" (Brennan 2004, 145–46).

"It" here is the id, which is part of the "faster 'I'" which here "thinks infinitely more rapidly." The "slower 'I'" here is called the secondary process, that which puts everything into words. And that "slower 'I'" is rushing to catch a train.

"Rushing" here is called "puffing to keep up." In this emphatically physical version, we see something inelegant, someone who does not have enough energy; someone who is running out of breath. That desperate, pathetic person who because she is rushing is puffing is here, by chance, a "middle-aged lady."

When I first read this passage, I thought I recognized the middle-aged lady as the familiar butt of jokes—a joke presumably made by someone younger and/or a man. The word "lady" in particular suggests that the writer is at some remove from the ludicrous figure. And it is the word "lady" which makes the "puffing" particularly funny. A lady should not have to rush; a lady should be waited for a lady should act like Teachout's elegant image of Teresa.

I was not comfortable poking fun at the poor lady, suspicious that it might be a sexist and/or ageist joke. Then I remembered something I have trouble remembering, that I am "a middle-aged lady." And then and only then, after I recalled something about myself I'd rather forget, did I remember that the writer of that sentence was likewise "a middle-aged lady."

Teresa and I were the same age. Thus I take the liberty of imagining that if my identification with the puffing middle-aged lady made me wince, Brennan might have had a similar relation to that unattractive figure.

Rushing and slow—the worst combination; desperately rushing to catch up with something "infinitely more rapid." That middle-aged lady puffing is an image for the difficulty of putting rapid thoughts "into words," an image for the laboriousness of writing. It is a self-portrait of the writer struggling to write—an image of extreme difficulty, if not impossibility; an image which could bring us back to those two epigraphs and the fear of not having enough strength and energy to put thoughts into words.

—◦⟨⊚⟩◦—

The middle-aged lady puffing is not where I had intended to end this paper. My plan was to end on the glamorous image of Teresa never once rushing. Yet twice in this paper, I found myself moving from a lovely, reassuring image of Teresa in the foreword into the book where I find a more anxious, troubled Brennan.

I want to end on something lovely and neat, precisely because Teresa has died and I am writing to honor her. But as much as I want to honor Teresa, I want more to honor Brennan. Whereas "Teresa" in this paper refers to the woman I knew, "Brennan" is meant to signify the author of the works I am reading. I can only honor Brennan by reading the book she wrote.

The lovely images in Teachout's foreword are there because Teresa is dead. But the images in the book are Brennan's images, put there by the writer who was alive and writing. When I move from the neat, elegant images in the foreword into the more troubled and troubling images in the book, I feel I connect to a mind that is thinking, struggling, alive, writing. In that middle-aged lady puffing, I feel I can catch a glimpse of Teresa Brennan, not so elegant perhaps, short of breath to be sure, but still breathing.

References

Brennan, Teresa. 2004. *The Transmission of Affect*. Ithaca: Cornell University Press.

———1992. *The Interpretation of the Flesh: Freud and Femininity*. London: Routledge.

Freud, Sigmund. 1955 [1920]. *Beyond the Pleasure Principle*. Vol. 18 *Complete Psychological Works*, trans. James Strachey. London: Hogarth.

CHAPTER ELEVEN

Can We Make Peace?*

For Teresa Brennan

———⁓⊙⊙⁓———

Julia Kristeva

Translated by Shannon Hoff

THE PREMATURE DEATH OF Teresa Brennan fills me with an immense sadness. I have lost a friend—one who introduced me into the circle of Hannah Arendt's collaborators and accomplices at the New School, and who could always inspire me with the interest and pertinence of her thought in the domains of femininity, of the sacred, of psychoanalysis. In these moments of grief, it is very difficult to interpret her thought, to reflect and continue the debate. I can only collect myself, reminisce about her, invite all to read and re-read her, and dedicate to her the text presented as part of the Universal Academy of Cultures, at the UNESCO in Paris in December, 2002.

Can we make peace?

"Peace, peace! When there is no peace." Thus spoke Jeremiah, the "prophet of doom," opponent of lies, of false prophets and idolaters who began to prophesize around 627–626 B.C. It was at this time that Deuteronomy was promulgated, Babylon triumphed over Syria, Nebuchadnezzar began his campaign against Jerusalem, and the first deportation took place—as did the plunder of Jerusalem, the captivity in Babylon and the migration of a number of Jews to Egypt: "For they have healed the hurt of the daughter of my people slightly,/ Saying 'peace, peace!'/When there is no peace" (Jeremiah 8:11).

---

* Julia Kristeva originally delivered this essay as a session paper at the Sixth International Forum of the Universal Academy of Cultures on December 20, 2002 in Paris, France.

Today you ask me if we can make a peace that does not exist. I think of the famous "peace process" of which there remain only disastrous tatters, a legion of "preventions," "sabotages," "quagmires," "standstills," and other "killings." I think of the state of latent war, the so-called situation of "insecurity," into which terrorism has plunged the world since September 11, 2001, and which was announced long before this fateful day in the big metropoles and in our suburbs by economic misery, the failures of integration, and the ravages of fundamentalism.

I am not unaware that "we are making peace" in Paris, and even in New York—that in spite of the oil slicks floating in the Atlantic, nature remains relatively beautiful, that the men and women of the third millennium continue to have children, they contemplate the sunsets and greet the birds of the fields, breathe the flowers at their windows, savor good wine and fine dishes, and dream of the future. I mean to say that for even the most fortunate, today peace seems beyond endangered—a vision of the mind, perhaps even a hallucination, like a transparent film, an evanescent perfume, the wing of a bee, the dream of a sage who imagines himself a butterfly, or of a butterfly picturing itself as a sage. I ask myself if peace was ever before beset by as many "principles of precaution," if not incredulity. And I wonder.

Suppose peace only existed as an object of belief, faith, and love. That is, what if it only existed as an imaginary discourse? This would mean that it possessed some reality, even a definite reality. It suffices to read a novel, see a film, listen to a CD, or participate in a religious rite for this imaginary reality to take hold of us, if only as project or promise: "That peace be with you and with your spirit;" "Amen;" "We depart in peace under the law of silence." Appeasement is an imaginary process: It drives destructive passions to express themselves in words, sounds, and colors; symbolic productions replace the daily conflicts and wars in order to compose a neo-reality, which is an ideal—often even an idyll, always a sublimation of violence—that we receive as beauty, as a fragment of serenity or peace.

The Catholic mass, among many other rites, is a paroxystic example of this appeasement, which made even Marcel Proust dream, when the writer defined every form of art as a "transubstantiation." He understood by this word that not only the bread and wine changed into the body and blood of Christ, but that their assimilation in the act of consumption—original violence if there ever was any—procures for the communicant a state in which he finds himself fulfilled, once more serene and appeased. If he elaborated through fantasy the murderous impulses in the imaginary, if he assuaged in reverie the violence of the sword and blade, tamed the chasms of darkness, sounded the depths of the alchemical vessel, avoided the snares of the mosaic square, and more, then the officiant of the rite can go in peace, provisionally, in the real world, which is supposed to provide liberty, equality and fraternity.

The analytic process is itself, a means of "making peace": It disrupts the logic of the elaboration-sublimation of aggression for which the religions before us have, precisely through fear, paved the way, making use of terror while promising purification.

In the beginning is hate, says Freud in essence, in counterpoint to the assessment (how much more reassuring) according to which "In the beginning was the Word." Nevertheless, although it seems more pessimistic, Freud's assertion was not entirely so for even as he recognized the significance of the "death drive," which has motivated kamikazes throughout history, the founder of psychoanalysis no less proposed a possible imaginary appeasement, defined by him as an analysis, which, while certainly "interminable," presents an opportunity to stubbornly and continuously disband the grip of mortality. In this way the analysand *can make peace* in himself and with others, indefinitely! How do we accomplish this miracle? The invention of the unconscious was the first step, it has been said, toward the creation of this "chimera" that is the *analytic session:* a place that is imaginary, symbolic, and, if it succeeds, real—where the analyst and analysand regress to their most unspeakable drives in order to succeed, from these states of reciprocal depersonalization, in clearing new paths. Murders, culpabilities, and vengeances are transformed in this way into psychic rebirths, into new lives.

Whether in religion, art, or psychoanalysis, these alchemies of appeasement cannot but entail major risks, and the fire of the death drive with which they play is only kept at bay by the creation of artifices: We only make peace by entrenching ourselves in social and historical reality, by protecting the imaginary process in the enclosure of the "sacred," the "aesthetic," or the "therapeutic" itself. We know only too well the frequent outbursts of these "delimited spaces" which, not content to stir up the fratricidal conflicts within their own spheres, trigger wars of all kinds in the "secular" world itself, unless they make accomplices therein.

More than other religions and beliefs, the monotheisms that marshal the initiatives of their Subjects, far from confining themselves to sacred space and its extra-temporality, integrate or insinuate themselves into the course of History and more or less brutally direct it. We are forced to recognize that it is by the grace of Christianity, especially of its secular descendants, that the *discourse of peace* left the domain of the private or collective imaginary to claim realization in the social reality of men and of women, in their families, clans, and nations. For that, it was required that the morality stemming from the Bible be supplanted by a *universalist word* (parole) *amorous of singular life*. Neither Jews nor Greeks—we are all sons of God and, in an echo of the cosmopolitanism of the Greek stoics, peace can only exist in this condition. This is what "universal fraternity," whose abuses and impasses we know only too well, proclaims, but which is henceforth the explicit condition of all progress in social peace: "Blessed are the peacemakers, for they shall be called sons of God" (Mt. 5:9). Whatever its Greek or Jewish antecedents (the Eros of myths and Plato, or the Biblical Song of Solomon), Christian love, *agape* or *caritas*, carried the good news, which still remains a message of fraternity. However, anticipating as always the "users" of politics, artists and philosophers did not delay in discerning its ambivalences and pitfalls.

When Kant's practical reason proclaimed *Perpetual Peace*, his celebrated text of 1795, it was not only a rejoinder to the revolutionary Terror, but even more a political translation of the evangelical message, logically based on universalism and the love of human life. Was not Pope John Paul II the statesman the most (and perhaps the only) concerned to invoke, not Kant, but the "rights of man" that inspire them both, not without permitting himself—"à la guerre comme à la guerre"—the notorious exceptions that suit him? This source of the modern morality that I call "imaginary" (I understand the word "imaginary," as you know, in the gravity of its intrapsychic and intersubjective reality) founds the rights of man today and, since the founding text of *Perpetual Peace*, has continued to reveal itself.

All the while proposing, very reasonably, to assure peace by the project of a "federalism [that] should eventually include all nations and thus lead to perpetual peace,"[1] and all the while envisaging not less reasonably to recognize the *differences* at the very heart of this Republic of peace, Kant wonders what could properly be the foundation of a morality capable of inspiring the respect of linguistic and religious differences in the universal peace he envisages; a morality that would be capable of transcending the limited needs of national and religious politics. The modern reader is left astonished to find no other foundation for the peace Kant demands than the necessity of guaranteeing the survival of the species on, alas, the limited surface of our earth: "For since the earth is a globe, they cannot scatter themselves infinitely, but must, finally, tolerate living in close proximity, because originally no one had a greater right to any region of the earth than anyone else."[2]

We cannot, however, reduce Kant's thought to a prescription for peace following exclusively from "natural constraint." In fact, if the species in its entirety must obtain the exercise of rights for all and over all, within the bounds of our earthly condition, if we are "naturally" constrained to peace on account of the limited rotundity of our earth, it is because this "natural constraint" is founded on two implicit pillars: First, that of universality—all men are equal and all must be saved; second is the principle of the protection of human life, sustained by the love of the life of each.

The modern detractors of what they call the "*droit-de-l'hommisme*"[3] are mistaken in thinking that the Rights of man (*Droits de l'homme*), the foundation of imaginary peace, reveal their fragility in the simple fact that universalism has failed to administer social justice. It is true that all men are not "equal and universal brothers" as long as economic, racial, and religious exclusion can banish them from society or deprive them even of hope. Yet whatever the weaknesses, the efforts for realizing social, economic, and political justice have never in the history of humanity been as considerable and widespread. It is the second pillar of the imaginary of peace that seems to me today to suffer most gravely: The love of life eludes us; there is no longer a discourse for it.

I say therefore that peace is in crisis—in Gaza, Jerusalem, Paris, New York, differently and conjointly—because *we are lacking a discourse on life at the beginning of this third millennium.*

Yet, who does not feel profoundly attached to *this* one of these "values," itself in crisis: namely, to life? We hardly know what we mean by the word, however, save perhaps the *need* to prolong it with the least suffering possible. Even then, suicidal or sadomasochistic drives are not lacking in some of "life's" intense excitations. Much more than in the "*clash* of civilizations," the deficiency of modern civilization resides in our lack of response to the question: What is a life? What does it mean to "love life"? Since scientific and rational democracies do not themselves possess a discourse for this fateful line of questioning, should we be surprised to see religions become the release mechanisms of the death drive? This death drive that they have for the purpose of keeping company with violence, and which they flatter themselves on curbing, forbidding, and sublimating! Such is the state of the world today, and it is not favorable to "making peace."

Confronted with the two totalitarianisms of Stalin and Hitler, Hannah Arendt declared both to be part of the same "evil," which asserts the "superfluousness of human life" by assuming the right to eliminate particular human groups from the face of the earth: Jews, Tziganes, the mentally ill. On their heels the philosopher distinguishes between "zoea" or biological life, and "bio" or recounted life (biography)—sharing in the memory of the City with other living beings, not necessarily with the most heroic, brilliant, or outstanding, but with ordinary people, with anyone, provided that he is respected as an emerging subject. In memory of Saint Augustine, Hannah Arendt, the Jewish German philosopher of the American language, saluted the "miracle of natality," for she saw in it the ontological foundation of liberty: It is because we are born free and transient that the world can be saved from its ruin, if not capable of "making peace."

> Human action, like all strictly political phenomena, is bound up with human plurality, which is one of the fundamental conditions of human life insofar as it rests on the fact of natality, through which the human world is constantly invaded by strangers, newcomers whose actions and reactions cannot be foreseen by those who are already there and are going to leave in a short while (Arendt 1954, 61).

Scientific investigations on the biological frontiers of life notwithstanding, we are forced to recognize, according to Hannah Arendt, that we do not have a discourse on the "meaning of life," and even less so on the "love of life."

Since the modern epoch elaborates its "amorous discourses of life" in the novel, let us see what the French novel has to offer: erotic exploits that pose as rivals of the sacred through the innocence of minimalist writing—when it is not in a dull form, in a modern variant of ironist deception; toxic regressions to fragments of the "primitive scene" and beneath that, to a memory without a representation of the species; a nostalgia for great centuries and great men (rarely great women!) who left us orphans—that is, lacking objects and projects, unless they are that trite form which is the soap opera, scandalous yet spectacular, in the American style. The novel, which emerged at the end of the Middle Ages as an account of amorous life, does not, at least in the wild versions of the market of the spectacle, recount anything today but the ruins of life and the modern psyche.

It is the very regime of the spectacle that radically changes the reality of what was in the past an "aesthetic object," at the same time as it changes our relation to it. Social and sexual promiscuity, the apparent openness of custom, the mix of backgrounds and classes, the crisis of prohibitions that diminishes when it does not sweep away the sense of modesty, the secret, and even intimacy, have contributed to and furthered this situation. Thus the barrier between, on the one hand, the "free association" that Freud offered us at the end of the nineteenth century in an attempt to reveal and adjust the destructiveness of the unconscious, and, on the other, the market of aesthetic products, is destroying itself between the more or less "unrefined" "bio" and the seduction of the Beautiful; between the hell of drives and the paradise of sublimation.

The television screen that affords us familiarity with (or makes us *believe* we can be familiar with, in this case the difference matters little) the familial and sexual intimacy of X or Y. We know (or believe we know, in this case the difference matters little) that the fairy tale that He or She describes for us in his novel is a denial of his anguish of death, of the anguish of death inspired in him by the death of his mother or, closely related, his mistress, and that He or She succeeds in denying in order to fill in his hell with a sublime paradise. You say "aestheticization of life"? A false idyll, rather, which denies, or contents itself with mocking, the complexities of life.

I know, you know, because you have had them on the couch, X and Y who have suffered traumatic incest and produced books from the experience that so resemble the discourse on the couch it is difficult to tell them apart: direct, untransposed confessions that like to think they are the "truth itself," the quintessence of the "I," the finally authentic "subject" that no longer troubles itself with style, rhetoric, and other imaginary and inevitably outdated displacements, but that cries out in a bewitching logorrhea for the other patients—all the spectators not yet analyzed or in the course of analysis—which is, as everyone knows, interminable. In this way, therefore, the victim of incest (strengthened by his analysis? We can imagine!) succeeds where the paranoiac fails: in incarnating The Truth; and, armed with the whip of his powerfully phallic discourse, in transforming the literary spectacle into a fight, to the greatest pleasure—or profound ennui, it all depends—of spectators who can do nothing about it, and who won't be long in dropping off to sleep.

I know, you know, because you have heard their confessions, directly or through friends and acquaintances, or because you have seen various "shows," that the "sexual life" of X and Y is a dramatic *taking action* that counterbalances—for the time being and forever—their infantile psychosis, in these *happenings* or confessions that serve not as group psychotherapy but as narcissistic support; *that* may be done, that is permitted, I am neither man nor woman, but servant of the giant Sex around which congregates the community of officiants. A community of swingers, but also an extended community consisting of the audience of my analyst, my editor's acceptance of my story, the fascination that my discourse exerts on the market, et cetera. Why would you want me to know more? That which I know of sex and my unconscious is considerably enough to live by—to maintain a certain identity, avoid suffering, enjoy a spectacular recognition—ah, yes!—any bidders?

I do not evoke these phenomena solely to draw your attention to the transformation of the regime of the "beautiful" in contemporary society. Neither do I do so to pose the question of the role of psychoanalysis in this change. Messenger of truth as it is, is not psychoanalysis, when it is vulgarized and ceases to be experienced as a *process without end,* exploited as an alibi for fetishism, narcissistic complacency, and the general perversion of discourse and behaviors? More gravely, it is concerned with the modern representation of the meaning of life.

We could "encode" or "filter" porn films and other violent media as much as we want, but no restoration of the prohibition will withstand the reign of the society of the spectacle, or a life in which meaning is banally choked in pleasure for pleasure's sake. In this logic, the truth of pleasure is nothing other than death, and the truth of life is the same. We are very far from peace, save that of cadavers, depleted as they are of needs and sensual pleasures (*jouissances*). The sexual liberation of advanced democracies has led us either to a precautionary return to the amorous ideals and life plans of days of old, or to borderline experiences in which psychic space is parceled out, when not totally nullified, and ceded to the *new maladies of the soul:* violence, addiction, criminality, or psychosomatic suffering. If some manage thereby to imprison or shelter an always provisional peace, this idyll is only possible in the isolation of the aesthetic act, or in the resurgence of more or less eclectic religious communities on the margins of institutional concord.

It is not prohibition that we lack in this life that evades peace: The enthusiasts of "full security" are as numerous and determined as their symmetrical opposite—those who advocate "unbridled pleasure." It is the bond to life that is still pending. Not the innocent life, which the voluntarist moral doctrine believed threatened by the exiguity of our spherical earth alone. Rather, the life that cohabitates with the violence of desire, which myths, religions, the post-romantics, Nietzsche, Freud, and others have revealed to us, before and after Kant: life—a violent desire nevertheless susceptible to imaginary sublimation.

Making peace? This would be to transform the desire of death between the same and the other into a harmony among differents. This hypothesis is rooted in the dramatic and delicious cohabitation of the two sexes, is distilled in the friendship between them and celebrated in the peace that presides over the birth of a new life. It is not a coincidence if the crisis of the *discourse of life* took the appearance of a crisis of amorous discourse, and that it experienced its paroxysm throughout the second half of the twentieth century in the feminist demand, which, in its optimistic version, engaged in the liberation of the "second sex," and in its dogmatic form disclaimed maternity and the man-woman couple itself. Has feminism been a ruse of an emancipatory history moving toward parity through sinuous detours that fail to "make peace"? Or must we see in it a precursor of the dissolution of the vital bond from which we suffer today?

Let us pose the question, then, in this way: Is political discourse able to "make peace" in a world exposed to the primary drives such as the nuclear man-woman bond? It seems that a new division is emerging in the political realm today. On the one hand, there are those who understand humanity to be unfathomable, shunted about between life and death, and believe that politics must also face up to the abyss already tackled by anthropology, psychoanalysis, religions . . . On the other hand, there are those who, grasping at the brink of the abyss, try to protect their superficial administrative positions on the right as on the left.

Current Muslim fundamentalist intransigence is no stranger to this *crisis of the word* (parole) *of life* that democracies—boosted by technological development and dominated by the race for want and profit—are suffering, even if economic and political conditions pronouncedly different from ours overdetermine it and thus conceal its gravity from us. That Islam, opposed to suicide, could have become a cult of death in the name of sacrifice to God, should not be a surprise. Christianity also had its martyrs, and it was for the love of God that the Crusaders sacrificed themselves on the way to Saint Sepulchre. The triumph of this culture of death, disguised behind an appeasement promised beyond, reaches its height in the figure of the kamikaze: the *shahida*. [4] Originally destined for procreation, that is, for *zoea* and never for *bio*, women are sent off to sacrifice and martyrdom in imitation of the warlike man and possessor of power, which contemporary inquiry shows is a violation of Islam's own principles. It is especially the amorous disasters—pregnancy outside of marriage, sterility, desire for phallic equality with the man (like the Russian woman-nihilists who committed suicide for the Revolution)—that influence the vocation of *shahidas*. Some currents of classic Islam do not hesitate to pander to this alleged "equality" between the sexes, without ever envisaging the sexual and subjective *difference* of the woman, revelator of new life values and creativity! Fundamentalism dedicates those women of which it wants to rid itself to idealization and to the sacred cult. The amorous life of these women, with its intolerable and inassimilable novelties, marks the incapacity of the religious word (*parole*) to pacify the ambivalent bonds of free individuals, emancipated of archaic prohibitions but deprived of new justifications for their lives.

From Paris to Bali, and including Gaza, we are not at peace, for we only know how to object to life. In suggesting that the difficulty of "making peace" reveals the bankruptcy of life's imaginary, and of its hearth, amorous life, I do not want to merely invite you to consider the intimate face of politics. I want to point toward the *umbilicus* of that which we take to be a *clash* between civilizations and religions—which is, for everyone and differently, a bankruptcy of the vital imaginary. As the underside (*doublure*) of universal fraternity, the *desire for life*, and not the *need for its maintenance*, must be renewed if we want to revive the Kantian project of a peace to come.

From this perspective, it will not suffice to write the history of religions "into the program" in order to appease fratricidal beliefs and rival traditions and relieve a humanity entirely and finally moralized into universal tolerance. We must also recall that according to Kantian universal peace, thought, which is also writing, does not cease in opening new paths for the word (*parole*) of life and hatred; for the purpose of pacifying us indefinitely, provisionally. The economic and political response is not easy, but what we lack even more concerns the anthropological foundation, where the desire for life and the desire for death confront each other. Nevertheless, we have the power to leave the question open, for in closing it again we would condemn life as well as peace.

To prevent the closure of *this question* under the guise of the study of religions, let us attempt a provisional remedy: Let's inscribe them in programs that genuinely interrogate them—philosophy to begin with, and art and literature. Let us reread the verse of Jeremiah in this polyphonic context: "Peace, peace! When there is no peace!"

Like the prophet Jeremiah, I do not say to you, that it is impossible to make peace. Rather, peace is inaccessible here and now, because it is futile to impose by moral will an imaginary harmony that requires *justice* for universalism to be realized in the public realm, and requires, just as imperatively, a new discourse on the love of life, *bio* and not *zoea*, for intimacy to regain its serenity. How does each religion conceive of the project of life and the relation between the sexes that underlies it? More than the peaceful coexistence of religions, it is *a radical analysis of their logic of life* that can still save us.

But do we really want to be saved? "Peace, peace! When there is no peace!" The prophecy of Jeremiah can also be taken as an apocalyptic pronouncement. Here and now. Take heed.

Notes

1. Immanuel Kant, *Perpetual Peace,* trans. Ted Humphrey (Indianapolis: Hackett Publishing Company, Inc., 1983), 117.

2. Ibid., 118.

3. The phrase "*droit-de-l'hommisme*" is a pejorative term employed by detractors of the discourse of human rights. Tr.

4. Kristeva writes "la kamikaze," signifying the female version, and "shahida" is Arabic for "martyr," as well as a relatively common female name. Tr.

References

Arendt, Hannah. 1954. "The Concept of History." In *Between Past and Future: Eight Exercises in Political Thought*. New York: Penguin Books.

A Eulogy for Teresa Brennan

Susan Buck-Morss

Iᴛ ɪs ᴅɪꜰꜰɪᴄᴜʟᴛ ᴛᴏ ᴡʀɪᴛᴇ a eulogy for a friend who has had a public life and thus belongs to the public sphere. Personal loss evokes images that are not the least bit monumental. For me it is Teresa driving her car onto our snowy lawn, missing the driveway completely and almost landing in the kitchen. Or eating ice cream cones in tourist Cuba as her sarong unravels, her obliviousness to which frightens away the heckling men. Or her elated return from visiting the priest in Havana's cathedral, with whom she had been discussing liberation theology—Marx and God—a bright blue silk scarf on her red hair, and optimism beaming from her face. Or the sudden stop for a margarita in Palm Beach; the sudden swim in the ocean; the sudden desire to write. Or, the last time I saw her, turning up late for lunch at Boodles in London—she had gotten on the train in the wrong direction—and then ordering salmon and champagne, charming the waiters with a surplus of living attention. How do these warmly human, humorous moments help to memorialize a rigorous intellectual, dedicated political activist, celebrated author, and leading feminist-Marxist-Lacanian-Catholic theorist of the new millennium?

Ethics were crucially important to Teresa. But in her understanding they sprang from the life-drive, not the will to disciplinary control. That was her genius. It made her impervious to strategies of governmentality by which, under pretense of moral correctness, the minds and bodies of citizens are kept in line. Exposure to her unique blend of ethics and liberty was in itself a lesson in social emancipation. It was subversive and the authorities knew it.

Teresa Brennan's life was a scandal, to be sure, but not for the usual reasons. Rather, it was the simple reason that she made you believe in your dreams. And she did this in the most implausible way, by telling the truth about the disasters in the world that human beings themselves were perpetrating in the forms of military, social, and ecological devastation. What institution in Bush's America could tolerate her kind of honesty? She was vulnerable simply for being herself. She is, after death, still having this scandalous effect.

Here is an email I received in November 2004 from a stranger:

Dear Professor Buck-Morss:

I am contacting you since I know that you were a friend of Teresa Brennan . . . I am writing to you now because I have decided that action is more productive than despair after the results of this month's presidential election. I did not know Professor Brennan but I am familiar with her work and her goals for the future of America and the planet and I am certain that she would have been saddened and indeed horrified by the election outcome. The blatant disregard for the lives of people and the environment are a frightening prospect for us to contemplate over the next 4 years.

Dr. Brennan truly spoke with the prophetic voice that Cornel West has recently described (in Democracy Matters[1]) as necessary to save our democracy from the powers currently holding our fate in their hands. To simply quote one example of Dr. Brennan's prescience:

'It may be that the desire for cheap gas and profit will win out over the claims of unborn generations to come and those living in poverty now, in which case the U.S. will continue to attract odium to itself for arrogance; it may defer but not defeat a judgment which will worsen in proportion to the degree it postpones right action. Either way, judgment comes upon us through our hands.'[2]

My letter to you is a response to that call for "right action." I have never been an activist but I believe the crisis we are now facing calls us to new roles . . . I know that she had great faith in the idea of the public intellectual and I agree that scholars need to go beyond the classroom and speak and listen to our fellow citizens. In this spirit I am working on a proposal for a national public forum: America in the Age of Globalization & its Terrors . . .

The concept of globalization and its terrors was essentially missing from the 2004 campaign and the American public is poorly informed on this topic . . . I feel that an ideal approach would enlist media such as the Public Broadcasting System and National Public Radio in combination with our educational system and public libraries. I am thinking specifically of a series of programs hosted by someone like Bill Moyers who has an excellent history of engaging public intellectuals on such issues. Recordings of these programs would be made available free of charge to schools and public libraries to be used in discussion forums by teachers and other members of the community. A selection of experts from a wide variety of areas would be involved in the creation of these programs . . . It would be important to get political leaders from all levels of government to participate in and listen to these discussions.

What is at stake is the planet. What is needed is a re-direction for America and the World. Let this Forum be the beginning of a reversal of polices and actions, so that the next four years are not remembered as America's darkest hour, but rather as the beginning of HOPE.

Sincerely,
Randy Bond, Ph.D.

Teresa Brennan's Ph.D. program to train public intellectuals, instituted at Florida Atlantic University under her directorship as Schmidt Distinguished Professor of Humanities and Public Intellectuals, was tailor-made for Randy Bond. His vision was precisely Teresa's own when she planned the program that night, at dinner, after driving onto my snowy lawn. What an idea she had, and what courage to implement it at a public university in Florida with the backing of a largely Republican elite! But you have to understand something about Teresa Brennan. She did not think in terms of party partiality. She never drew boundaries between religion and reason. She refused all of the divisive binaries that for so many of us seem to create such formidable barriers to creative politics. She believed in people's potential for goodness— all people, no exceptions.

Randy Bond's proposal is both reasonable and inspired. He is absolutely right in his analysis as to what is needed in America today, and what the 2004 U.S. Presidential election did not address. I have tried to help him in implementing his proposal and I am failing. Teresa would not have given up. She would be on the phone for a week to lobby for his National Public Forum, calling every possible person with influence, no matter how famous and unreachable. She would have in fact upped the ante, trying to get the whole world involved. She too might not have succeeded. But by refusing to be realistic, by dreaming as big as humanity, she would have affected countless people, nudging them to return to their childhood faith and risk opening the wounds of broken dreams. It was this ability she had to touch our hidden hopes that caused us to smile and feel protected in her care.

Most like Christmas for me in Teresa's care was her enormous delight in my intellectual creativity. She nurtured this in me and many others, and she did it in a way that made you feel that you should be rewarded, indeed, pampered during the creative process—a room by the sea and undisturbed writing days as I finished my article "Hegel and Haiti,"[3] about which she was visibly enthusiastic.

Teresa Brennan was singularly lacking in the Protestant ethic. Sensory pleasure, not suffering was her preferred road to salvation. Encouragement, not competition was her dream of professional renown. She wanted it for herself and she gave it generously to others. How wonderful that was, and how rarely I have experienced it in my twenty years as an academic professor.

The sense of security she provided for creative, critical work was illusory. This was true for no one more profoundly than herself. She was unprotected from disappointment, collegial rejection, deception, and even betrayal. Her vulnerability produced paranoia and it caused her enormous pain. So she suffered after all. And as her friend, living with her through that suffering, you could not help but remain aware that Christmas-giving is not the way "daily life in the West" is organized. Sometimes you did not want to take part in her dreams any longer, as they kept opening wounds that had hardened if not healed. Standard professional emotionlessness seemed the lighter burden. It hurt less deeply.

And yet none of us can repress completely the desire to believe that reason, affect, emotion, and the life-drive might someday shape the organization of human affairs. The deeply despairing question is: Why do we not succeed? It is not a new question, but one that at times seems more urgent. This is such a time, and the public intellectual never has been more needed.

In the spring of 2004, hosted by Alice Jardine of the Harvard University Committee for the Studies of Women, Gender, and Sexuality, a group of friends, students and colleagues of Teresa met to celebrate her life and work. We were faced with a problem then, and it is mine with this writing. How do we prevent the memorializing of a life from being overshadowed by the death-drive? How do we give tribute without building monuments to Teresa, as intellectual authority too often carries with it intellectual submission? How do we insist that honoring intellectual greatness can be one with honoring irreverence and freedom? And how do we convince others that utopian thought is the most realistic thinking in our time?

Writing, like parenting, is an act of faith. Teresa Brennan's books will find their readers in constellations of reception that none of us can predict or control. Nor should we. But as a postscript to the power of the intellectual legacy her work will spawn, let me just say that her life, with all of its contradictions and complexities, is the most valuable lesson that she gave to me. I would urge others to search for such people in their own lives, and embrace them.

Max Ehrmann wrote a prose piece in 1927 called *Desiderata*, a verse of which was narrated as a protest song in the early 1970s. The verse was from this section:

Beyond a wholesome discipline,
be gentle with yourself.
You are a child of the universe
no less than the trees and the stars;
you have a right to be here.
And whether or not it is clear to you,
no doubt the universe is unfolding as it should.

Therefore be at peace with God,
whatever you conceive Him to be.
And whatever your labors and aspirations,
in the noisy confusion of life,
keep peace in your soul.

With all its sham, drudgery, and broken dreams,
it is still a beautiful world.
Be cheerful. Strive to be happy.
© *1927 Max Ehrmann*

Ehrmann was an Indiana lawyer and writer, son of German immigrants. His *Desiderata* has circulated in multiple contexts, from *Readers' Digest* to the websites of mystics. Adlai Stevenson had it at his bedside when he died. Hippies handed it out on street corners. Several weeks ago, on the island of Mayreau in the Grenadines, I saw the text of *Desiderata* printed in full and posted on the wall of a small church. I was embarrassed when its sentimentality brought on a sudden surge of tears, perhaps because the present political situation in my country seems to have dashed the hopes that the protest movement expressed half a lifetime ago.

The small church was under the care of the Catholic Priest, Mark de Silva, who was assigned to the island of Mayreau over a decade ago. During the years he taught himself about the nature and ecology of the island, and then shared his knowledge with members of the parish who eventually formed a grassroots activist group, the Mayreau Environmental Development Organization (MEDO). The executive committee of this non-governmental organization included, along with Reverend de Silva, two teachers, a restaurateur, two t-shirt vendors, and a fisherman. The group's contributions to the island have included reintroducing land turtles, installing water tanks for poor families, procuring laptop computers for the local school, and distributing seventy garbage bins to island households.

Their big challenge took place several years ago. MEDO became involved in a fight to preserve the neighboring Tobago Cays, a glorious coral reef with an archipelago of uninhabited islands (upon which slave-cultivated cotton plantations were once imposed), by saving this natural treasure from plans by an international hotel chain to create out of it a luxury resort. Having lobbied the Saint Vincent and Grenadines government for authorizing a Tobago Cays Marine Park dedicated to the protection of its fragile ecology, they took on the multinational tourism industry to stop resort development of the Tobago Cays, enlisting the help of the United Nations and other global organizations. At least for the time being, they have won.

I thought of Teresa Brennan, and wished she were with me. As to the outcome of this David and Goliath battle, she would not have been surprised.

Notes

1. Cornell West, *Democracy Matters: Winning the Fight Against Imperialism* (New York: Penguin, 2004).

2. Teresa Brennan, *Globalization and its Terrors: Daily Life in the West* (London: Routledge, 2003), xxi.

3. Susan Buck-Morss, "Hegel and Haiti," *Critical Inquiry* 26, no.4 (Summer 2000): 821–865.

Contributors

—⟨⟨⟩⟩—

GILLIAN BEER has recently retired as King Edward VII Professor of English Literature at Cambridge. Her books include *Open Fields: Science in Cultural Encounter* (1996), *Virginia Woolf: the Common Ground* (1996), *Arguing with the Past* (1989), *George Eliot* (1987), *Darwin's Plots* (1983, 2000), *Meredith: A Change of Masks* (1970), and *The Romance* (1970). She recently edited and introduced a new edition of Freud's *The Wolfman and Other Case Histories* (2003). She is a Fellow of the British Academy, for which she served as Vice-President from 1994 to 1996, and a Foreign Honorary Member of the American Academy of Arts and Sciences. She is at present President of the British Comparative Literature Association. She is General Editor of Cambridge Studies in Nineteenth-Century Literature and Culture and is on a number of journal advisory boards. She has been a judge for both the Booker and the Orange Prize for fiction.

SUSAN BUCK-MORSS is Professor of Political Philosophy and Social Theory in the Department of Government as well as the Director of Visual Studies at Cornell University. Her publications include *Thinking Past Terror: Islamism and Critical Theory on the Left* (Verso, 2003), *Dreamworld and Catastrophe: The Passing of Mass Utopia in East and West* (MIT Press, 2000), and *The Dialectics of Seeing: Walter Benjamin and the Arcades Project* (MIT Press, 1991). Buck-Morss serves on the Editorial Boards of the journals *Constellations*, *Cultural Values*, *October*, *Parallax*, and the *Journal of Visual Culture*.

DRUCILLA CORNELL is Professor of Political Science, Women's Studies, and Comparative Literature at Rutgers University. She has written numerous articles on contemporary continental thought, critical theory, grass-roots political and legal mobilization, jurisprudence, women's literature, feminism, aesthetics, psychoanalysis, and political philosophy. She is the author and editor of numerous books the most recent of which include *Between*

Women and Generations: Legacies of Dignity (2002, 2005), *Defending Ideals: War, Democracy, and Political Struggles* (2004), *Just Cause: Freedom, Identity, and Rights* (2000), and the edited volume, *Feminism and Pornography* (2000).

ROBYN FERRELL is Chair of the School of Philosophy and Gender Studies at the University of Tasmania in Boart, Australia. She is the author of *Copula: Sexual Technologies, Reproductive Powers* (SUNY Series in Gender Theory, 2006), *The Real Desire* (The Scandinavian Press, 2004), *Genres of Philosophy* (Ashgate, 2002), *Passion in Theory: Conceptions of Freud and Lacan* (Routledge, 1996), and the editor of *Cartographies: Poststructuralism and the Mapping of Bodies and Spaces* (Allen & Unwin, 1991).

JANE GALLOP is Distinguished Professor of English and Comparative Literature at the University of Wisconsin-Milwaukee. She is the author of eight books of which the most recent publications include, *Living with His Camera* (Duke University Press, 2003); *Anecdotal Theory* (Duke University Press, 2002); and *Feminist Accused of Sexual Harassment* (Duke University Press, 1997). She is the editor of *Pedagogy: The Question of Impersonation* (Indiana University Press, 1995). She has also published some fifty articles in anthologies of criticism and in various journals.

SUSAN JAMES is Professor of Philosophy at The Birkbeck School of Philosophy, University of London. She is the author of *Passion and Action: The Emotions in Seventeenth-Century Philosophy* (Oxford, 1997) and *The Content of Social Explanation* (Cambridge University Press, 1984). She is the editor of *Margaret Cavendish: Political Writings* (Cambridge Series in the History of Political Thought, 2003), *Visible Women: Essays on Feminist Legal Theory and Political Philosophy* with Stephanie Palmer (Hart Publishing, 2002), and *Beyond Equality and Difference* with Gisela Bock (Routledge, 1992).

ALICE A. JARDINE is Professor of Romance Languages and Literatures and of Studies of Women, Gender, and Sexuality at Harvard University where she has been teaching post-war literary and cultural theory, French and Comparative twentieth-century fiction, and Women's Studies since 1982. She is best known as the author of the groundbreaking work of feminist theory entitled *Gynesis: Configurations of Woman and Modernity* (Cornell, 1985). She is also the editor of numerous important collections of essays in cultural studies (e.g., *The Future of Difference, Men in Feminism, Shifting Scenes,* etc.) and one of the first translators of Julia Kristeva's work into English. Most recently, she has completed a novel entitled *Booming: A Millennial Memoir* and is currently working on a new book project: *Prophetic Voices: The 21st Century 1950s Style.*

JULIA KRISTEVA is Professor of Linguistics at the University of Paris VII and is also a practicing psychoanalyst. Her books include *Semeiotiké* (1969), *Revolution in Poetic Language* (1974, tr. 1984), *Black Sun: Depression and Melancholia* (1987, tr. 1992), *Time and Sense: Proust and the Experience of Literature* (1994, tr. 1996), and *The Sense and Non-Sense of Revolt* (1996, tr. 2000). The subjects of her early twenty first-century trilogy on "female genius" are Hannah Arendt (tr. 2001), Melanie Klein (tr. 2002), and Colette (in an as yet uncompleted work). She has also written two novels.

SHANNON LUNDEEN is Associate Director of the Alice Paul Center for Research on Women, Gender, and Sexuality at the University of Pennsylvania where she teaches courses in Women's Studies. She recently co-edited a volume with Mary C. Rawlinson entitled, *The Voice of Breast Cancer in Medicine and Bioethics* (Springer 2006) and is co-editor of the *Philosophy Today SPEP Supplement* Vol. 47(5) (2003). She has also translated work by Enrique Dussell. Her recent research examines the philosophical significance of the contemporary claims for right and recognition in legal and political contestations regarding same-sex marriage in the United States.

ANNE O'BYRNE is Assistant Professor of Philosophy at Hofstra University where she teaches contemporary continental philosophy and political philosophy. Her recent research includes investigations of embodiment, labor, natality, and immunity as ontological and political concepts. Her recent publications include, "Utopia is Here: the Revolutionary Thought of Baudrillard and Nancy," "Symbol, Exchange and Birth: towards a Theory of Labour and Relation," "The Politics of Intrusion," and "The Birth of a Political Theory: Kelly Oliver on Politics and the Body." She has also translated work by Jean-Luc Nancy and Marc Froment-Meurice.

KELLY OLIVER is W. Alton Jones Professor of Philosophy at Vanderbilt University. She is the author of seven books: *The Colonization of Psychic Space: A Psychoanalytic Social Theory of Oppression* (University of Minnesota Press, 2004); *Noir Anxiety* (co-authored with B. Trigo, University of Minnesota Press, 2002); *Witnessing: Beyond Recognition* (University of Minnesota, 2001); *Subjectivity Without Subjects: From Abject Fathers to Desiring Mothers* (Rowman & Littlefield 1998); *Family Values: Subjects Between Nature and Culture* (Routledge 1997); *Womanizing Nietzsche: Philosophy's Relation to "the Feminine"* (Routledge 1995); and *Reading Kristeva: Unraveling the Double-Bind* (University of Indiana 1993). She has edited several books, including *The Portable Kristeva* (Columbia 1998), *The French Feminism Reader* (Rowman & Littlefield 2000), and *Between the Psyche and the Social* (Rowman & Littlefield 2002). She has also edited special issues of *Hypatia: a journal for feminist philosophy* and *Studies in Practical Philosophy: a journal of ethical and political philosophy*.

KALPANA RAHITA SESHADRI is Associate Professor of English and Director of Women's Studies at Boston College where she teaches courses in Postcolonial Studies, Psychoanalysis, and Political Theory. She is the author of *Desiring Whiteness: A Lacanian Analysis of Race* (2000) and co-editor of *The Pre-Occupation of Postcolonial Studies* (2000). She has published articles on the intersection of psychoanalysis and race and postcolonial theory in journals such as *Cultural Critique, Ariel,* and *Discourse*. She is at present working on a book-length project on postcolonial ethics, death, and alterity tentatively titled *The Other Difference*.

CHARLES SHEPHERDSON is Professor of English at University at Albany, and Aristotelian Chair in the Liberal Arts at Saint Thomas Aquinas College. He is the author of *Vital Signs: Nature, Culture, Psychoanalysis* (Routledge, 2000) and *The Epoch of the Body* (Stanford, forthcoming). In 2003 Shepherdson was the William P. Huffington Scholar-in-Residence at Miami University of Ohio and in 2004, he held the Aristotelian Chair in the Liberal Arts at Saint Thomas Aquinas College in New York. He has written widely on contemporary continental thought and psychoanalytic theory and his work has had support from the Henry Luce Foundation, the Andrew Mellon Foundation, the National Endowment for the Humanities, and from the Commonwealth Center at the University of Virginia, the Pembroke Center at Brown, and the Institute for Advanced Study in Princeton. He is currently working on a book on esthetics and emotion, grounded in Sophocles's *Antigone*.

Index